script
JODY HOUSER

pencils
EDGAR SALAZAR

inks
KEITH CHAMPAGNE

colors
MARISSA LOUISE

lettering
NATE PIEKOS OF BLAMBOT®

front cover art by
KYLE LAMBERT

chapter break art by
ALEKSI BRICLOT

president and publisher
MIKE RICHARDSON

editor
SPENCER CUSHING

assistant editor
KONNER KNUDSEN

collection designer
PATRICK SATTERFIELD

digital art technician
ALLYSON HALLER

Special thanks to KYLE LAMBERT, and NETFLIX, including: SHANNON SCHRAM, ELLEN DENG, JESS RICHARDSON, and TARA SINCLAIR.

Advertising Sales: (503) 905-2315 | ComicShopLocator.com

STRANGER THINGS: SIX, November 2019. Published by Dark Horse Comics LLC, 10956 SE Main Street, Milwaukie, Oregon 97222.

This volume collects issues #1 through #4 of the Dark Horse comic-book series *Stranger Things: Six.*

Published by Dark Horse Books
A division of Dark Horse Comics LLC.
10956 SE Main Street
Milwaukie, OR 97222

DarkHorse.com | Netflix.com

First edition: November 2019 | ISBN 978-1-50671-232-1

3 5 7 9 10 8 6 4 2
Printed in Canada

Library of Congress Cataloging-in-Publication Data

Names: Houser, Jody, author. | Martino, Stefano, 1970- penciller. | Champagne, Keith, inker. | Affe, Lauren, colourist. | Piekos, Nate, letterer. | Briclot, Aleksi, cover artist.
Title: Stranger things / script, Jody Houser ; pencils, Stefano Martino ; inks, Keith Champagne ; colors, Lauren Affe ; lettering, Nate Piekos of Blambot ; front cover art by Aleksi Briclot.
Description: First edition. | Burbank, CA : Dark Horse Books, [2019] | v. 1: "This volume collects issues #1 through #4 of the Dark Horse comic-book series Stranger Things: The Other Side."
Identifiers: LCCN 2018053216 | ISBN 9781506709765 (v. 1 : paperback)
Subjects: LCSH: Comic books, strips, etc. | BISAC: COMICS & GRAPHIC NOVELS / Science Fiction. | COMICS & GRAPHIC NOVELS / Media Tie-In. | COMICS & GRAPHIC NOVELS / Horror.
Classification: LCC PN6728.S769 H68 2019 | DDC 741.5/973–dc23
LC record available at https://lccn.loc.gov/2018053216

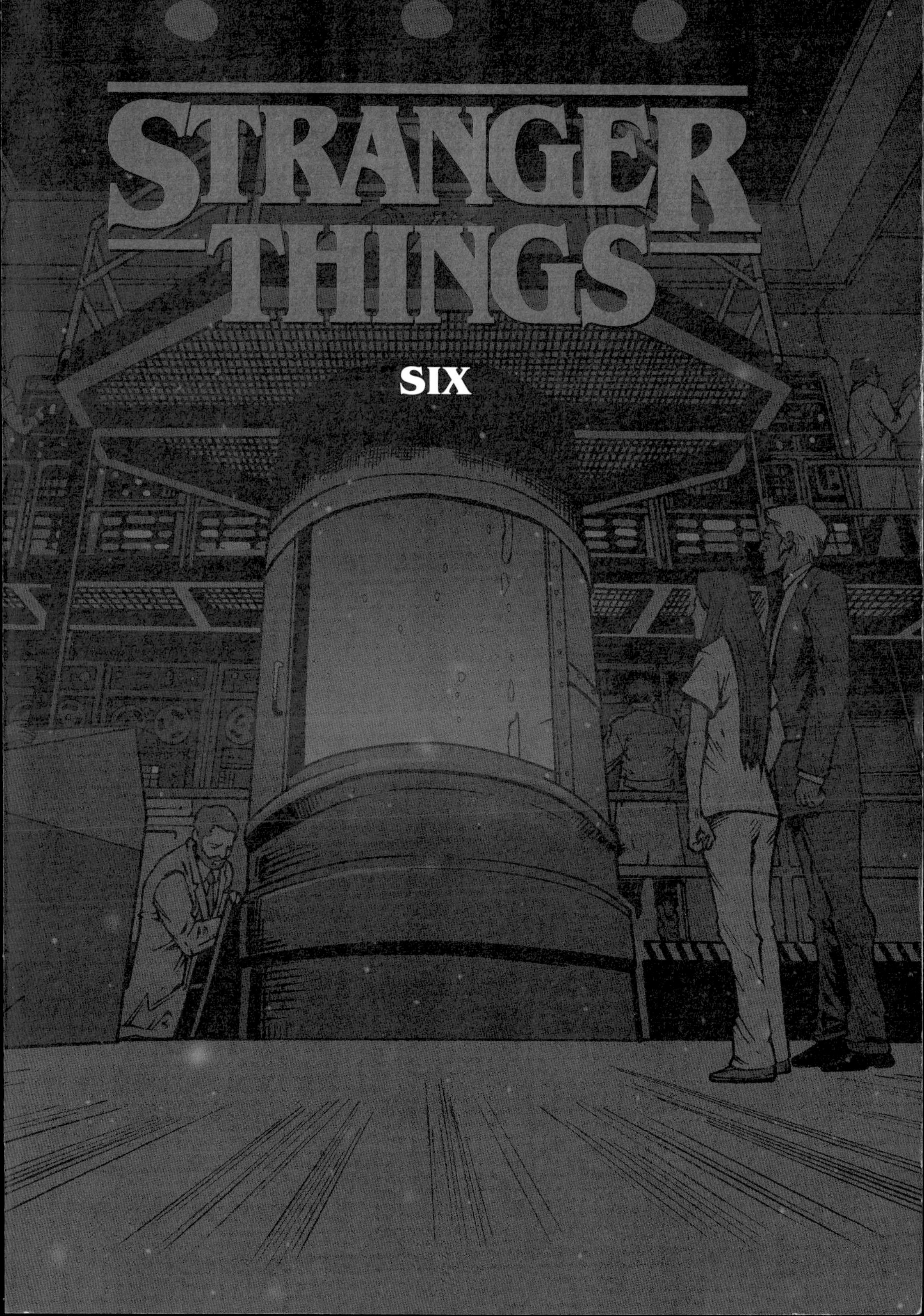
STRANGER THINGS
SIX

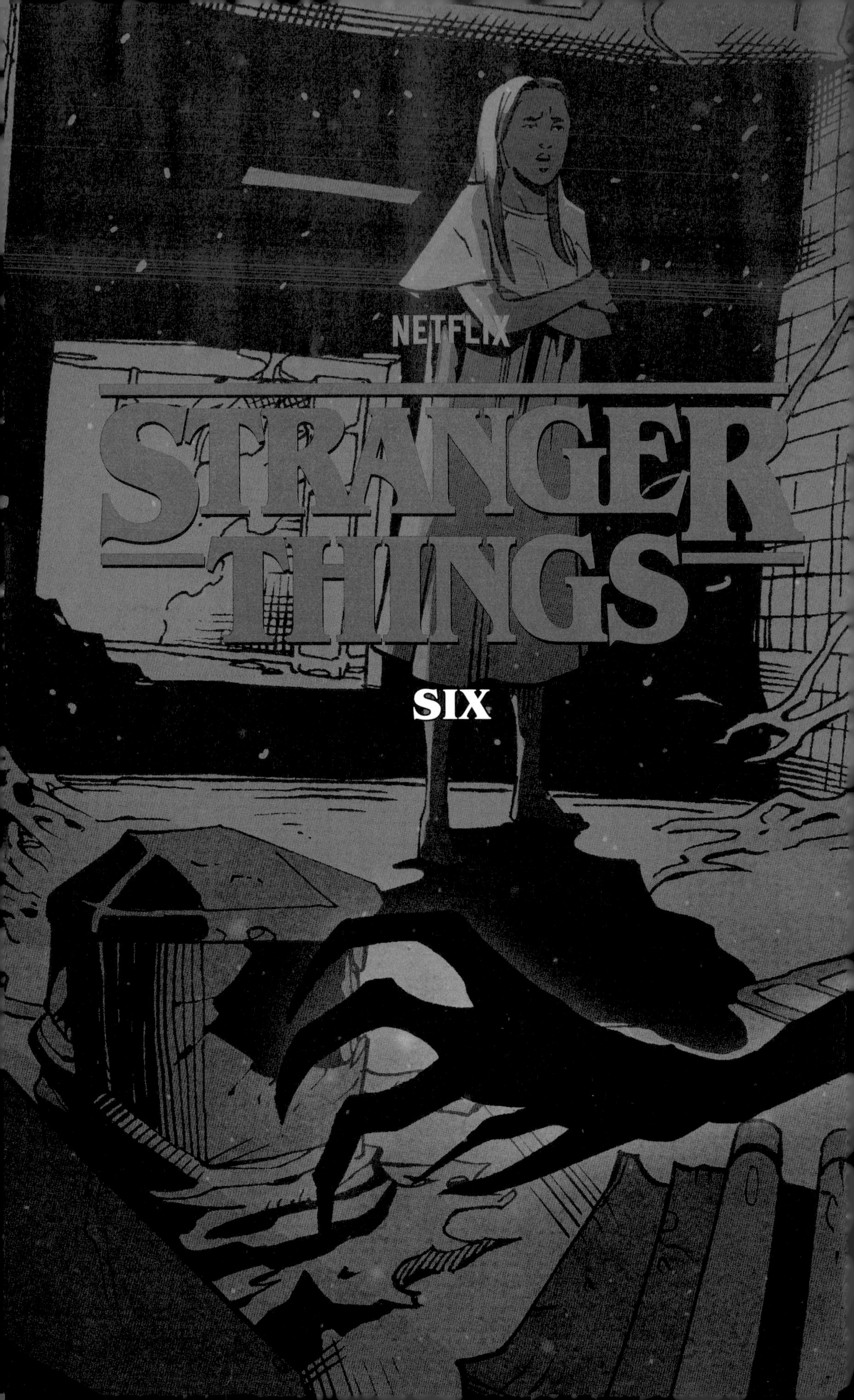
NETFLIX
STRANGER THINGS
SIX

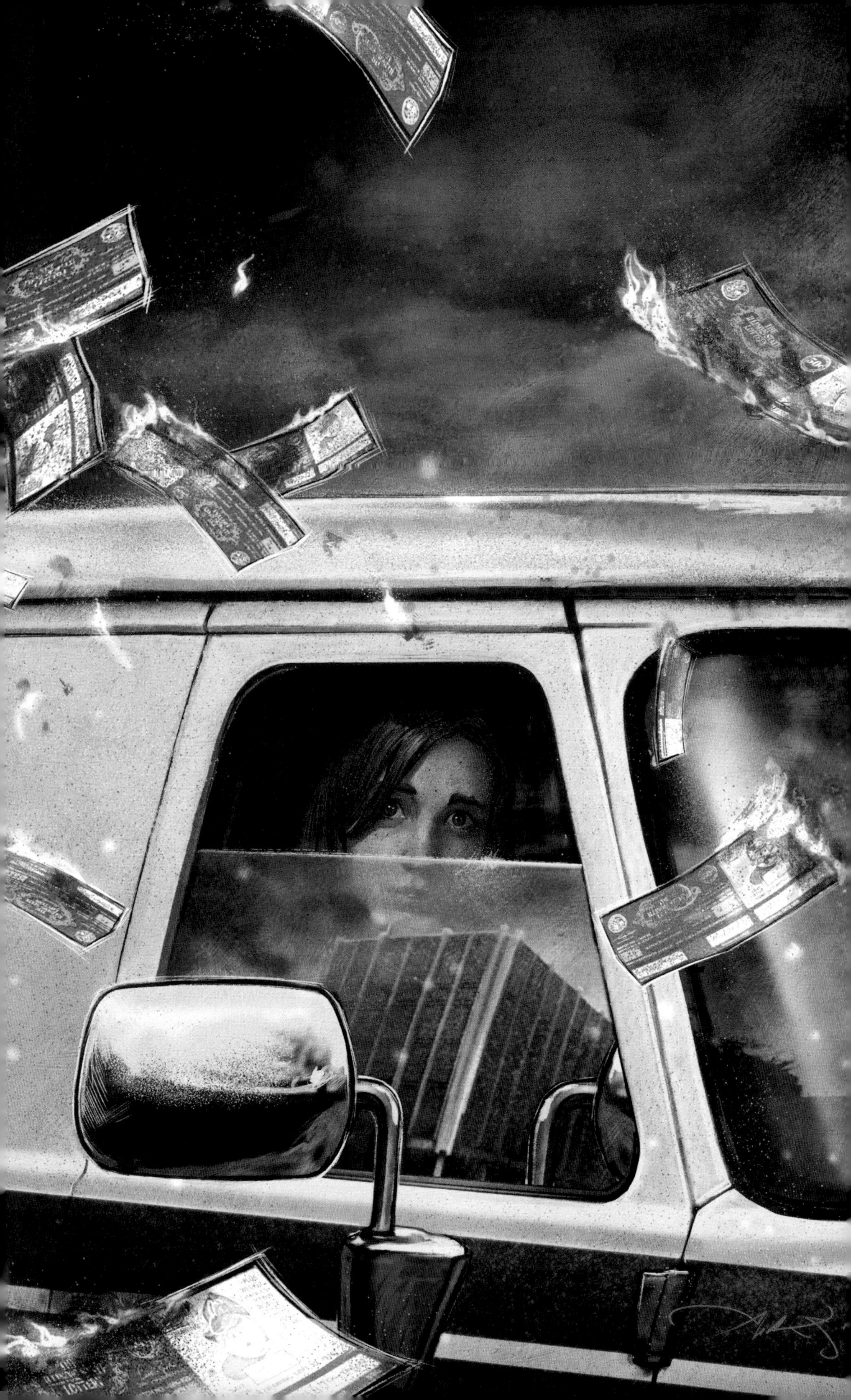

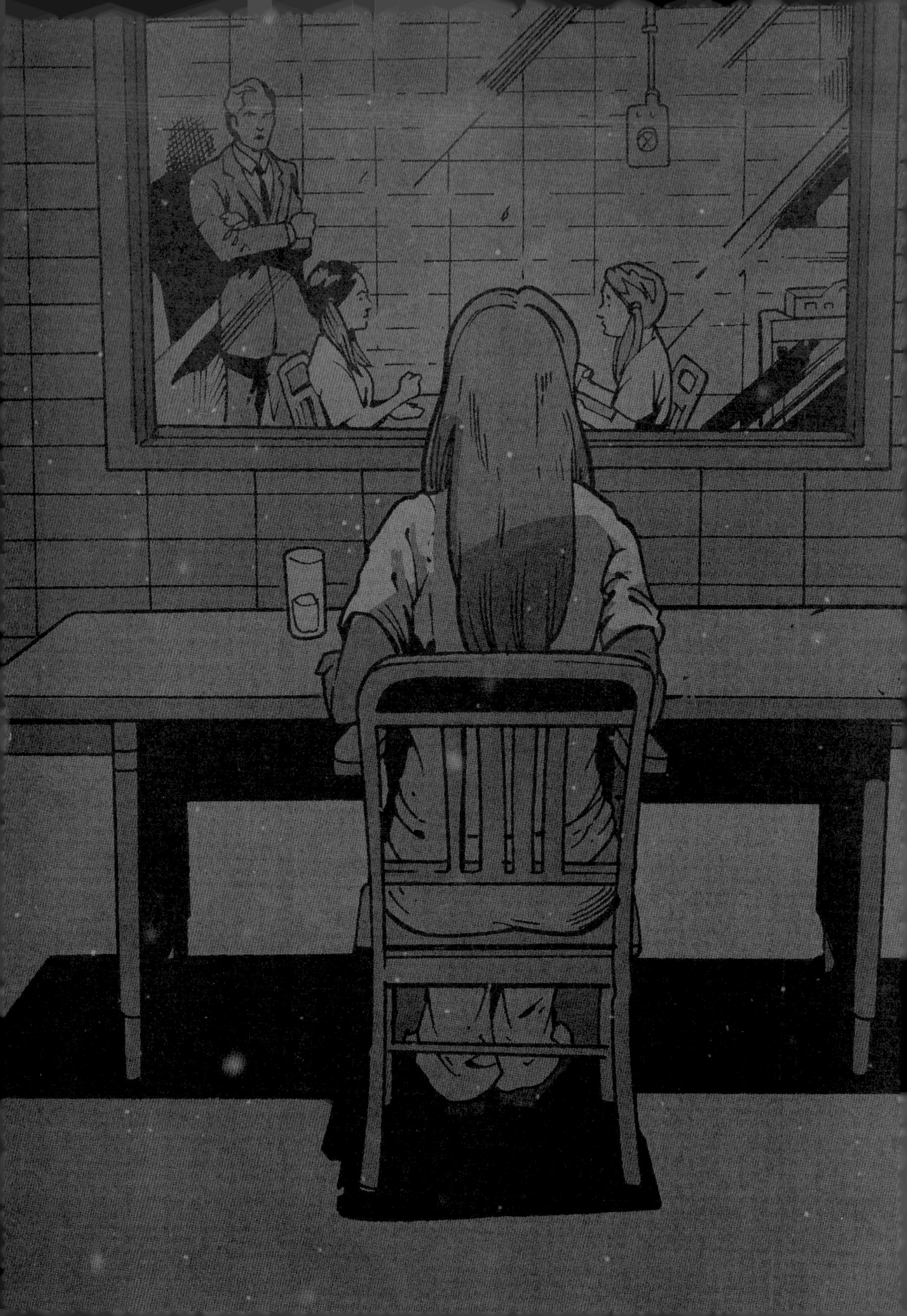

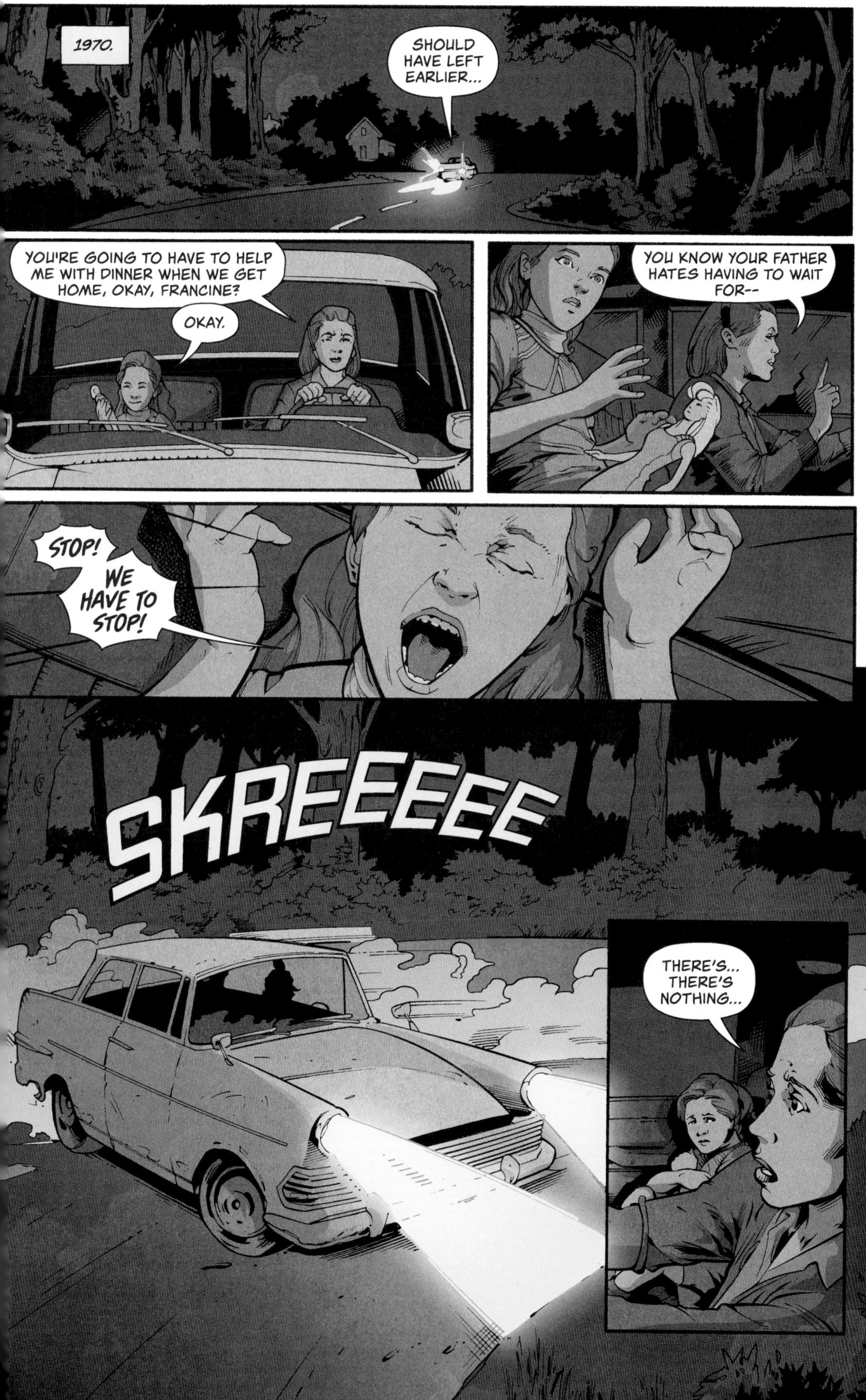
1970.
SHOULD HAVE LEFT EARLIER...
YOU'RE GOING TO HAVE TO HELP ME WITH DINNER WHEN WE GET HOME, OKAY, FRANCINE?
OKAY.
YOU KNOW YOUR FATHER HATES HAVING TO WAIT FOR--
STOP!
WE HAVE TO STOP!
SKREEEEE
THERE'S... THERE'S NOTHING...

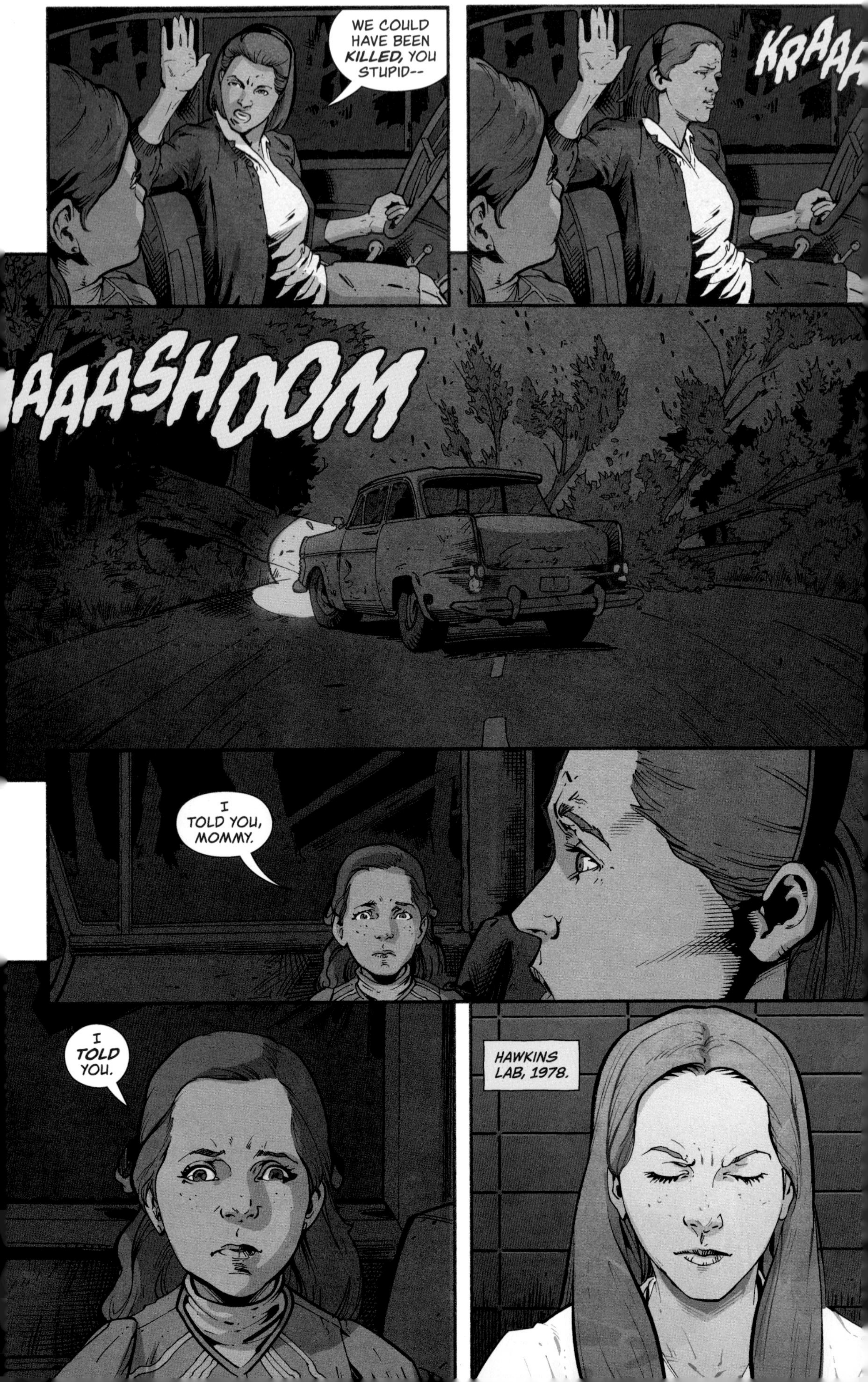
WE COULD HAVE BEEN KILLED, YOU STUPID--
KRAAA
AAASHOOM
I TOLD YOU, MOMMY.
I TOLD YOU.
HAWKINS LAB, 1978.

paper
cissors
cissors
aper
ock
rock
scissors
paper
paper
rock
paper
paper
rock
scissors
rock
rock
scissors
paper
rock
...TWO... AND THREE.
"SEVENTEEN PERCENT."

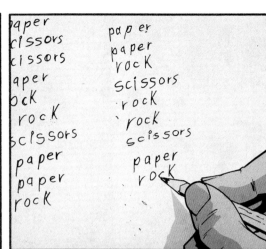

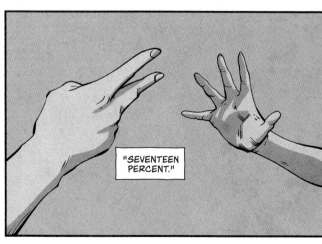

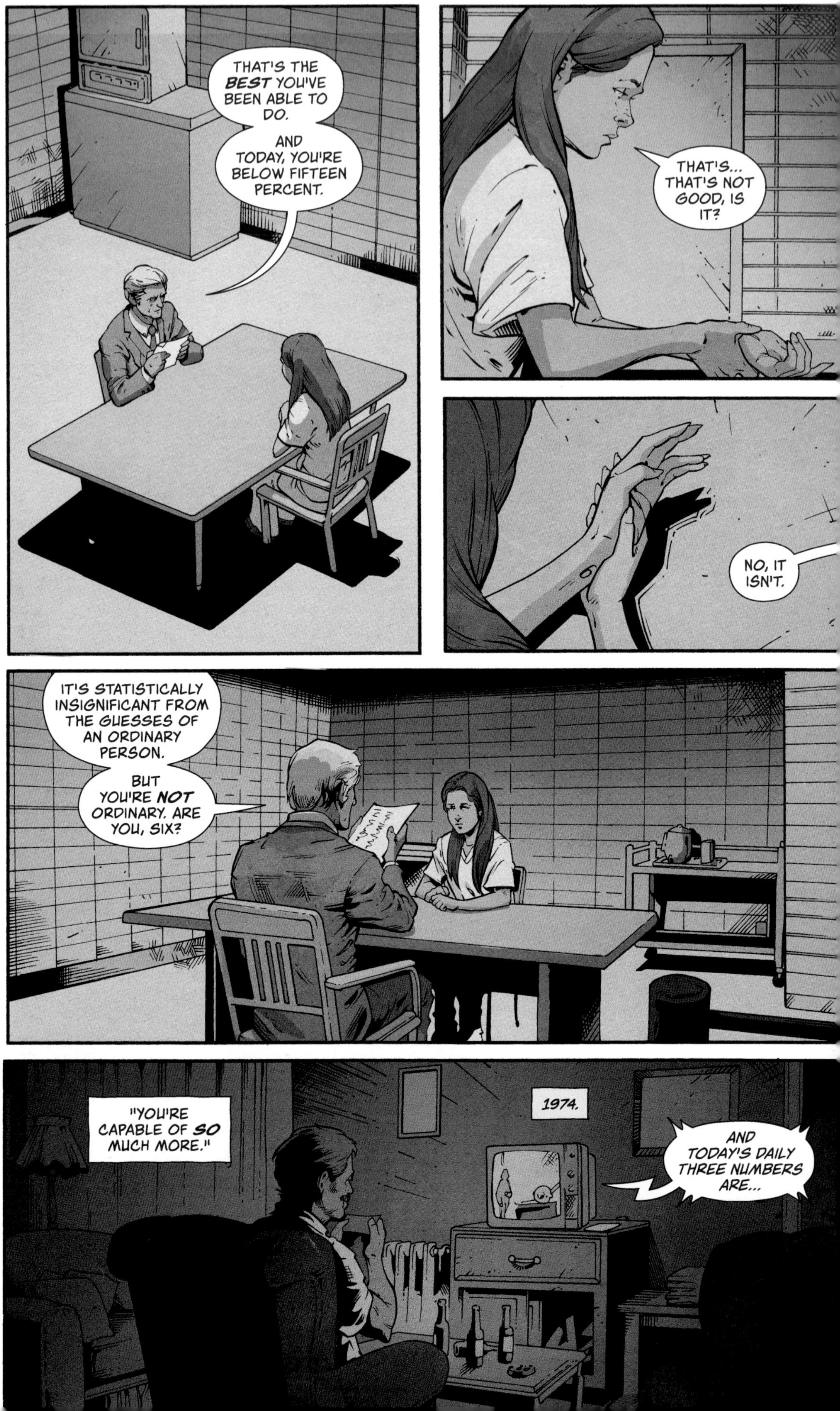
THAT'S THE BEST YOU'VE BEEN ABLE TO DO.
AND TODAY, YOU'RE BELOW FIFTEEN PERCENT.
THAT'S... THAT'S NOT GOOD, IS IT?
NO, IT ISN'T.
IT'S STATISTICALLY INSIGNIFICANT FROM THE GUESSES OF AN ORDINARY PERSON.
BUT YOU'RE NOT ORDINARY. ARE YOU, SIX?
"YOU'RE CAPABLE OF SO MUCH MORE."
1974.
AND TODAY'S DAILY THREE NUMBERS ARE...

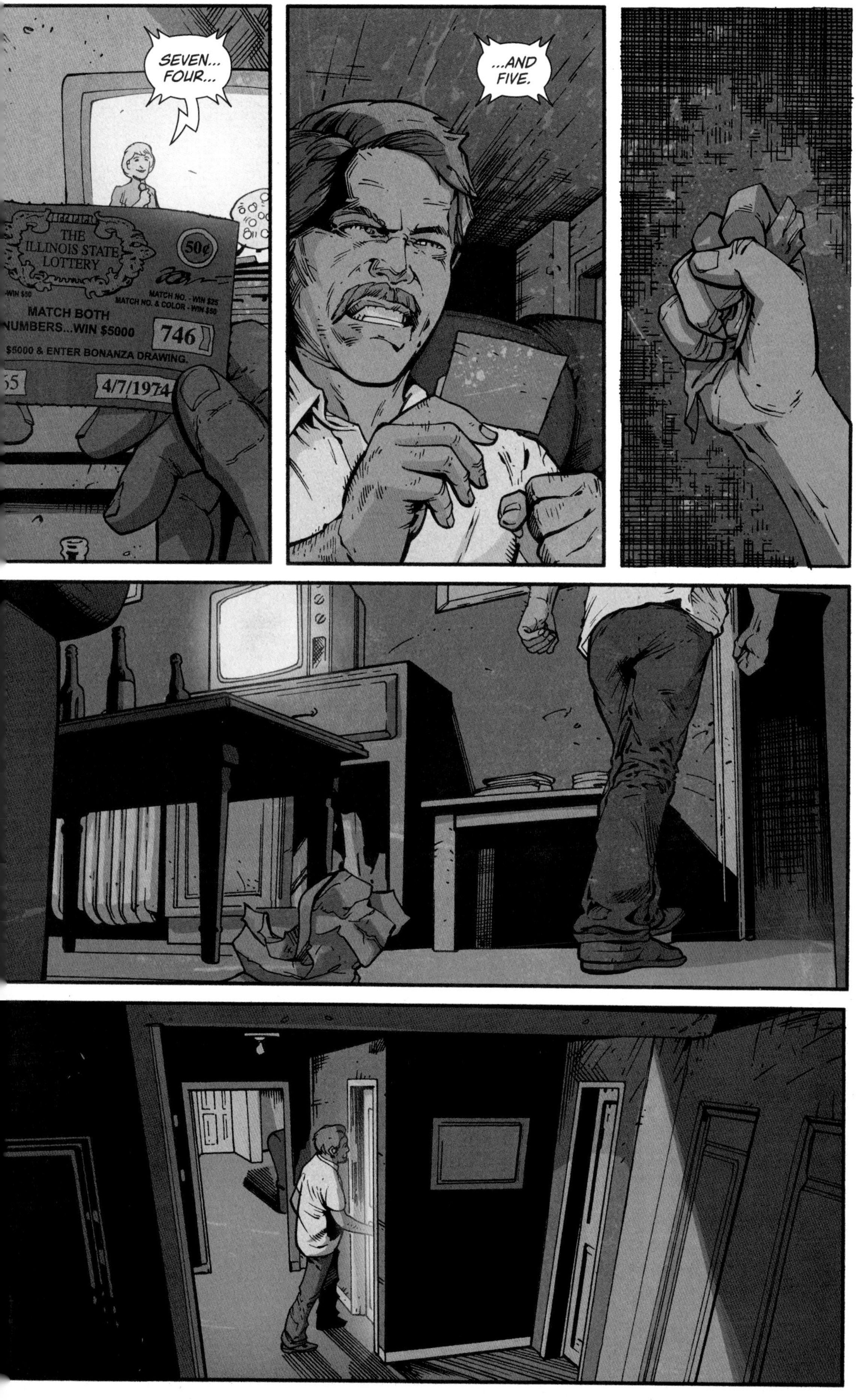
THE ILLINOIS STATE LOTTERY
50¢
MATCH NO. - WIN $25
MATCH NO. & COLOR - WIN $50
MATCH BOTH
NUMBERS...WIN $5000
746
$5000 & ENTER BONANZA DRAWING.
4/7/1974
SEVEN... FOUR...
...AND FIVE.

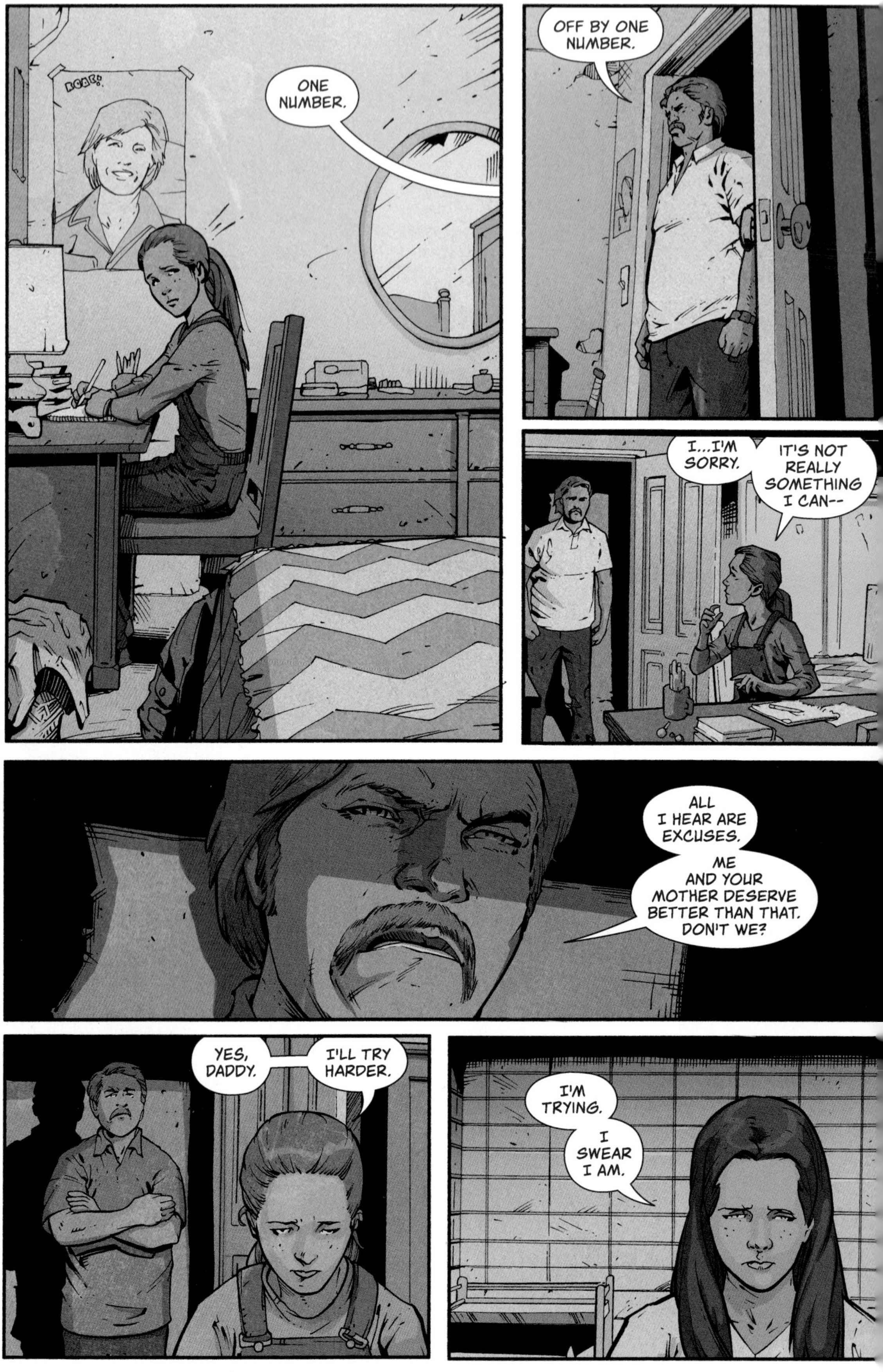
ONE NUMBER.
OFF BY ONE NUMBER.
I...I'M SORRY.
IT'S NOT REALLY SOMETHING I CAN--
ALL I HEAR ARE EXCUSES.
ME AND YOUR MOTHER DESERVE BETTER THAN THAT. DON'T WE?
YES, DADDY.
I'LL TRY HARDER.
I'M TRYING.
I SWEAR I AM.

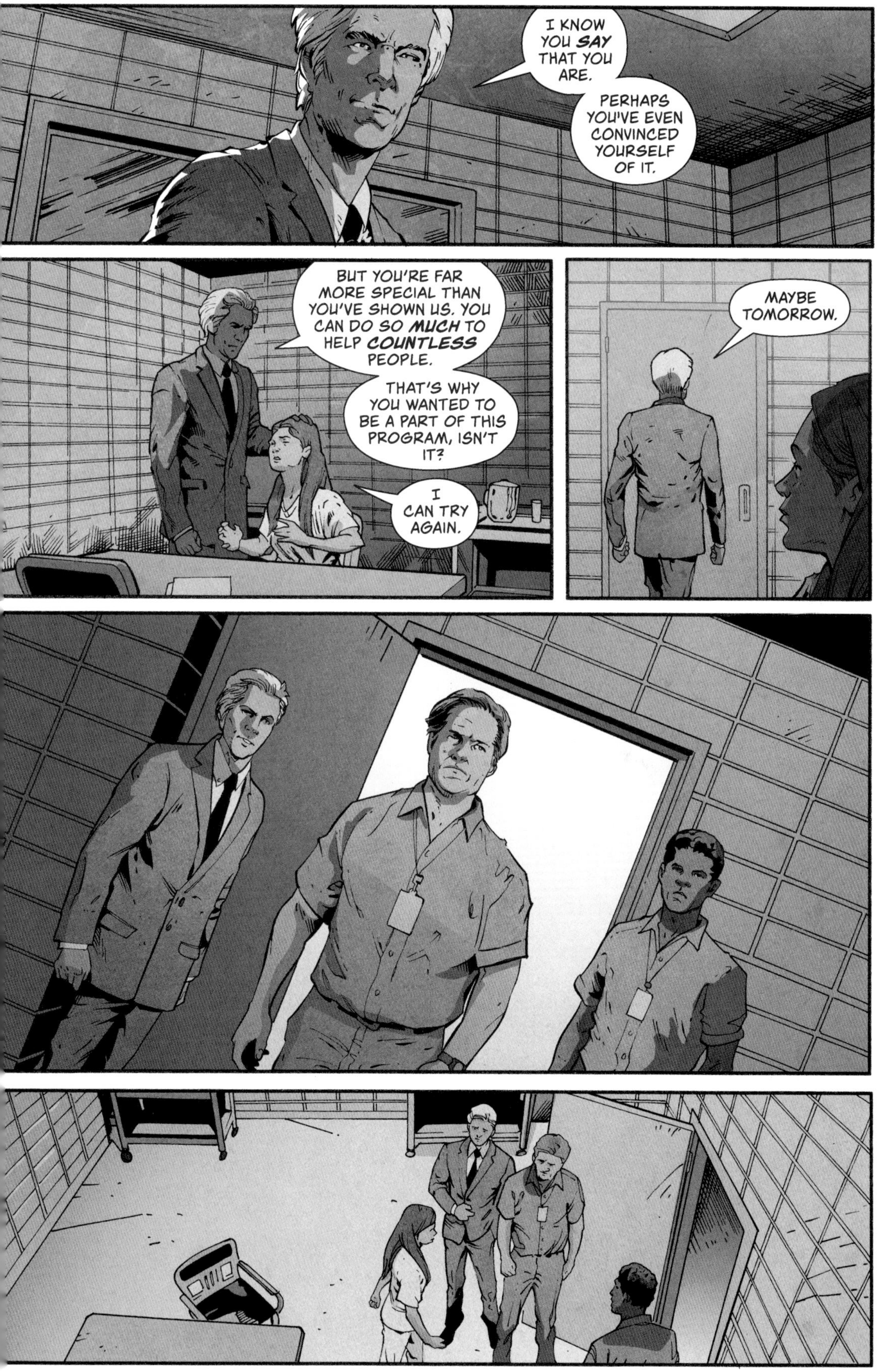
I KNOW YOU SAY THAT YOU ARE.
PERHAPS YOU'VE EVEN CONVINCED YOURSELF OF IT.
BUT YOU'RE FAR MORE SPECIAL THAN YOU'VE SHOWN US. YOU CAN DO SO MUCH TO HELP COUNTLESS PEOPLE.
THAT'S WHY YOU WANTED TO BE A PART OF THIS PROGRAM, ISN'T IT?
I CAN TRY AGAIN.
MAYBE TOMORROW.

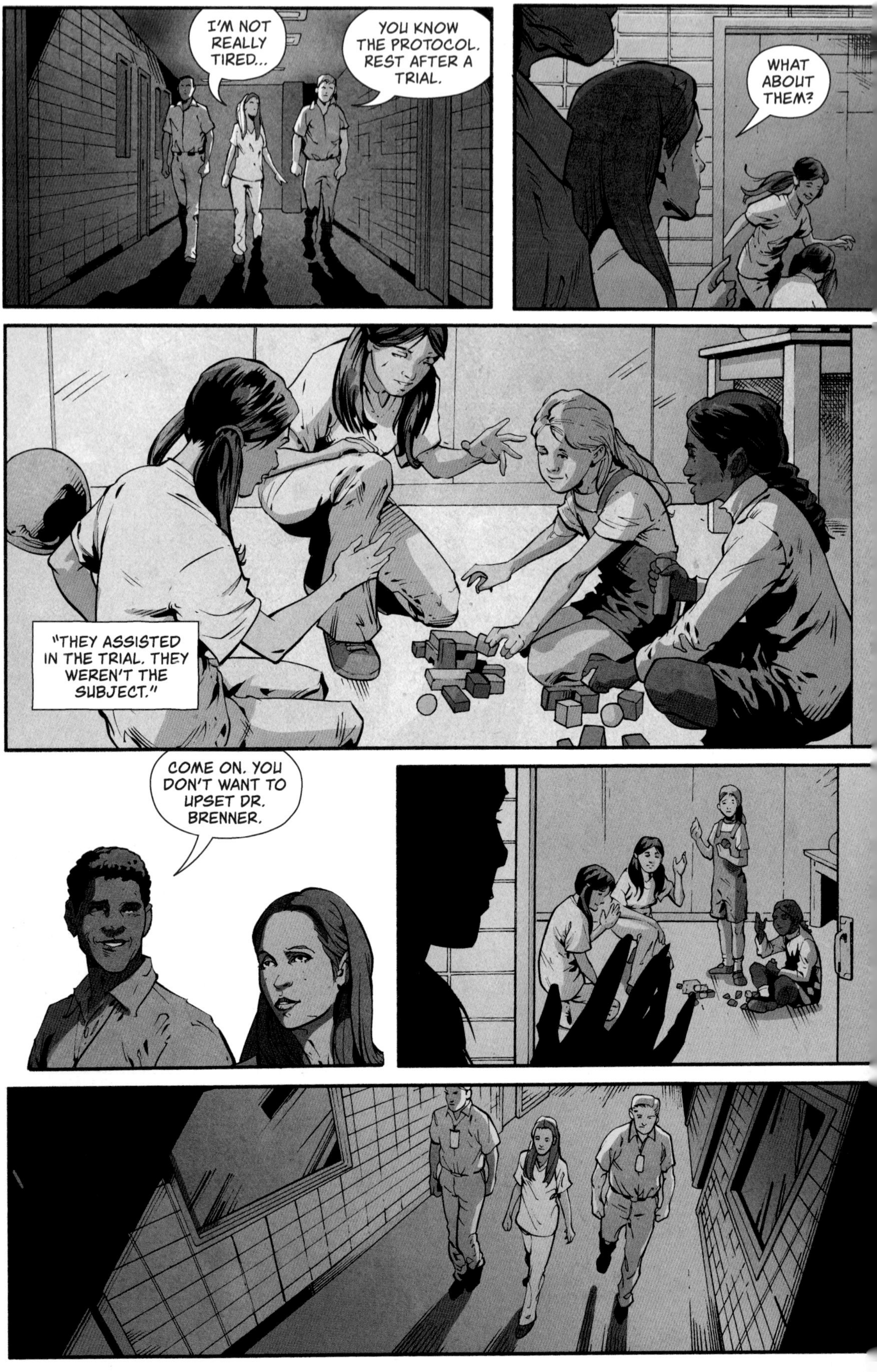
I'M NOT REALLY TIRED...
YOU KNOW THE PROTOCOL. REST AFTER A TRIAL.
WHAT ABOUT THEM?
"THEY ASSISTED IN THE TRIAL. THEY WEREN'T THE SUBJECT."
COME ON. YOU DON'T WANT TO UPSET DR. BRENNER.

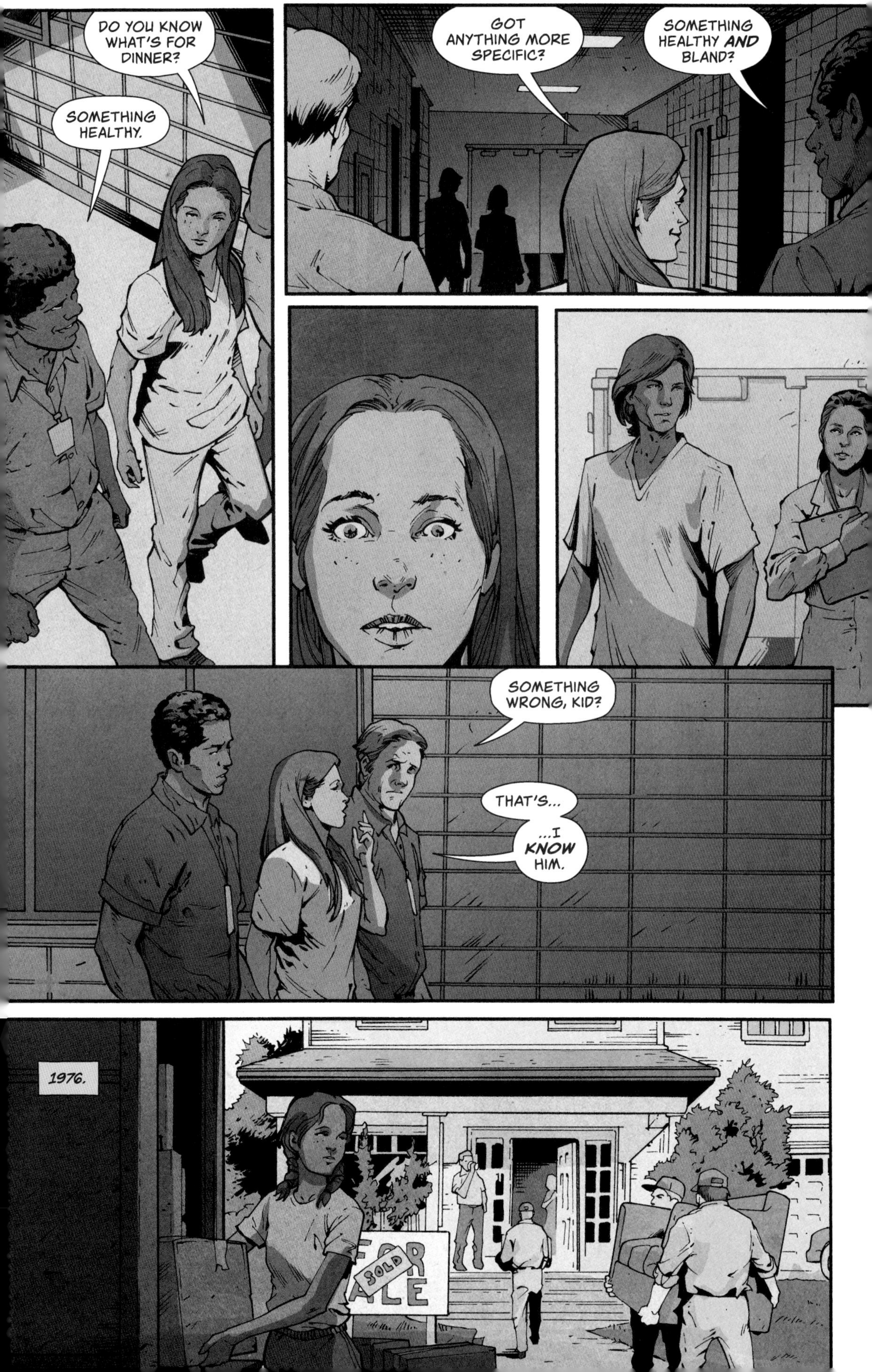
DO YOU KNOW WHAT'S FOR DINNER?
SOMETHING HEALTHY.
GOT ANYTHING MORE SPECIFIC?
SOMETHING HEALTHY AND BLAND?
SOMETHING WRONG, KID?
THAT'S...
...I KNOW HIM.
1976.
FOR SALE
SOLD

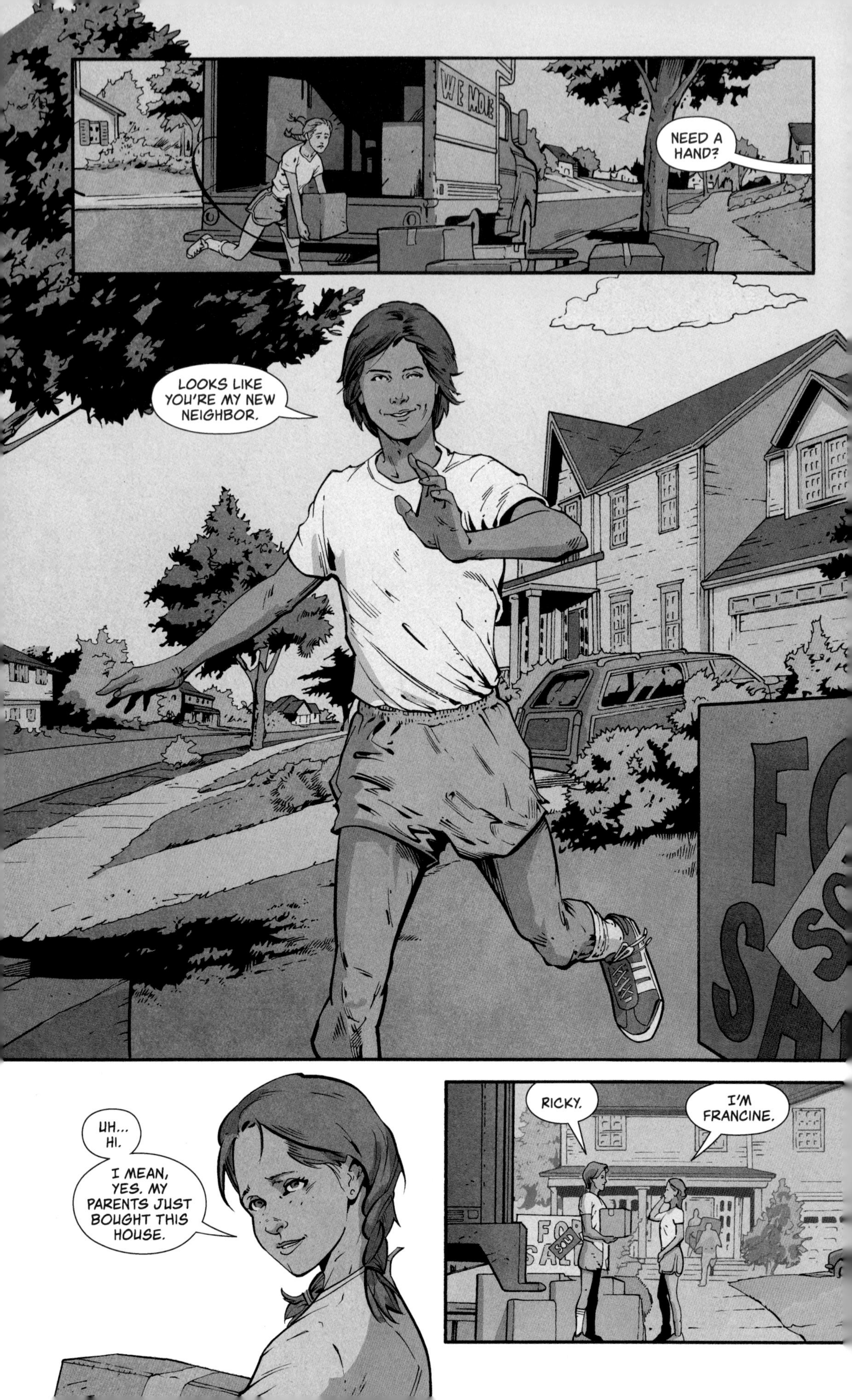
WE MOVE
NEED A HAND?
LOOKS LIKE YOU'RE MY NEW NEIGHBOR.
UH... HI.
I MEAN, YES. MY PARENTS JUST BOUGHT THIS HOUSE.
RICKY.
I'M FRANCINE.

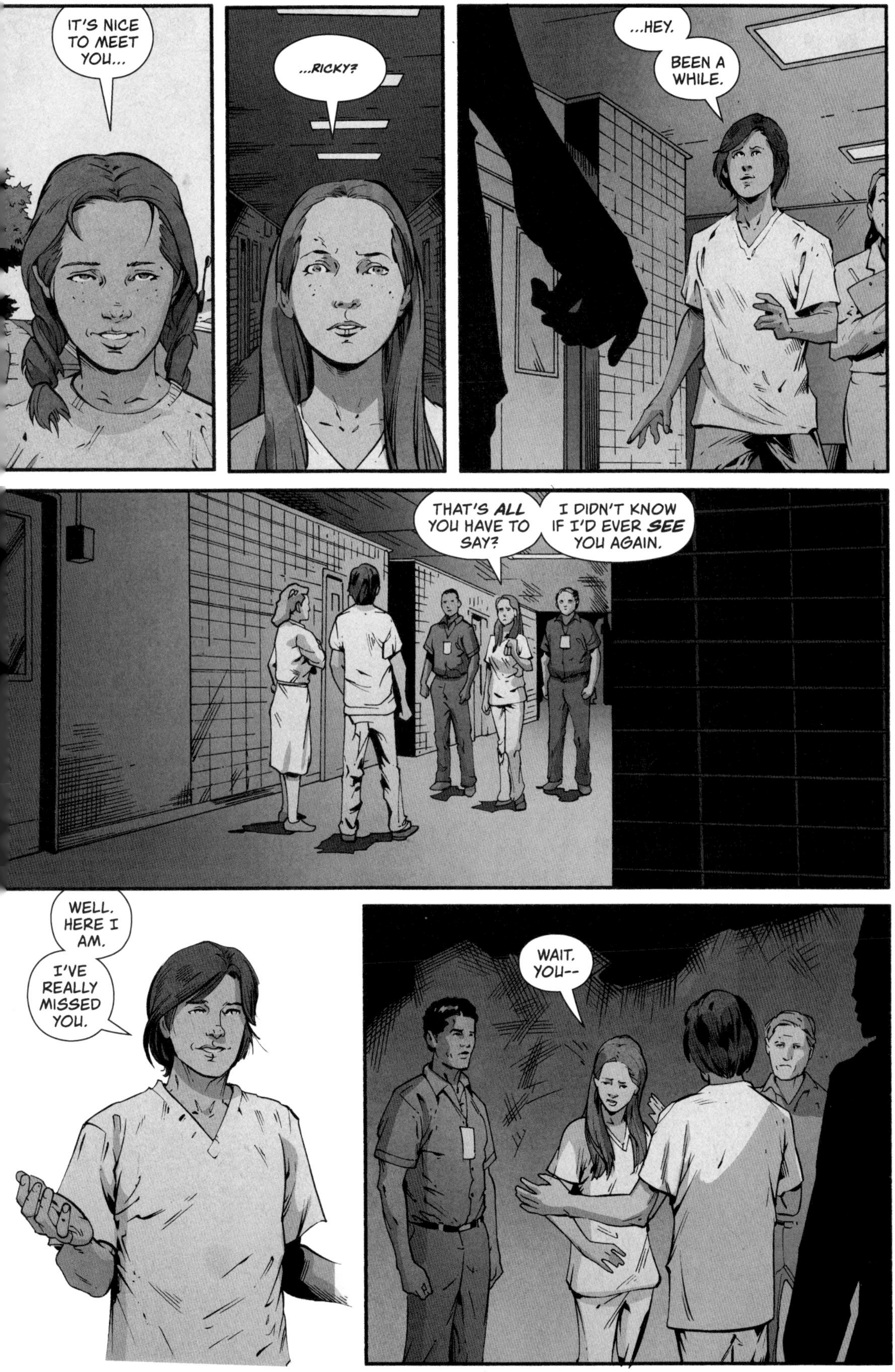
IT'S NICE TO MEET YOU...
...RICKY?
...HEY.
BEEN A WHILE.
THAT'S ALL YOU HAVE TO SAY?
I DIDN'T KNOW IF I'D EVER SEE YOU AGAIN.
WELL. HERE I AM.
I'VE REALLY MISSED YOU.
WAIT. YOU--

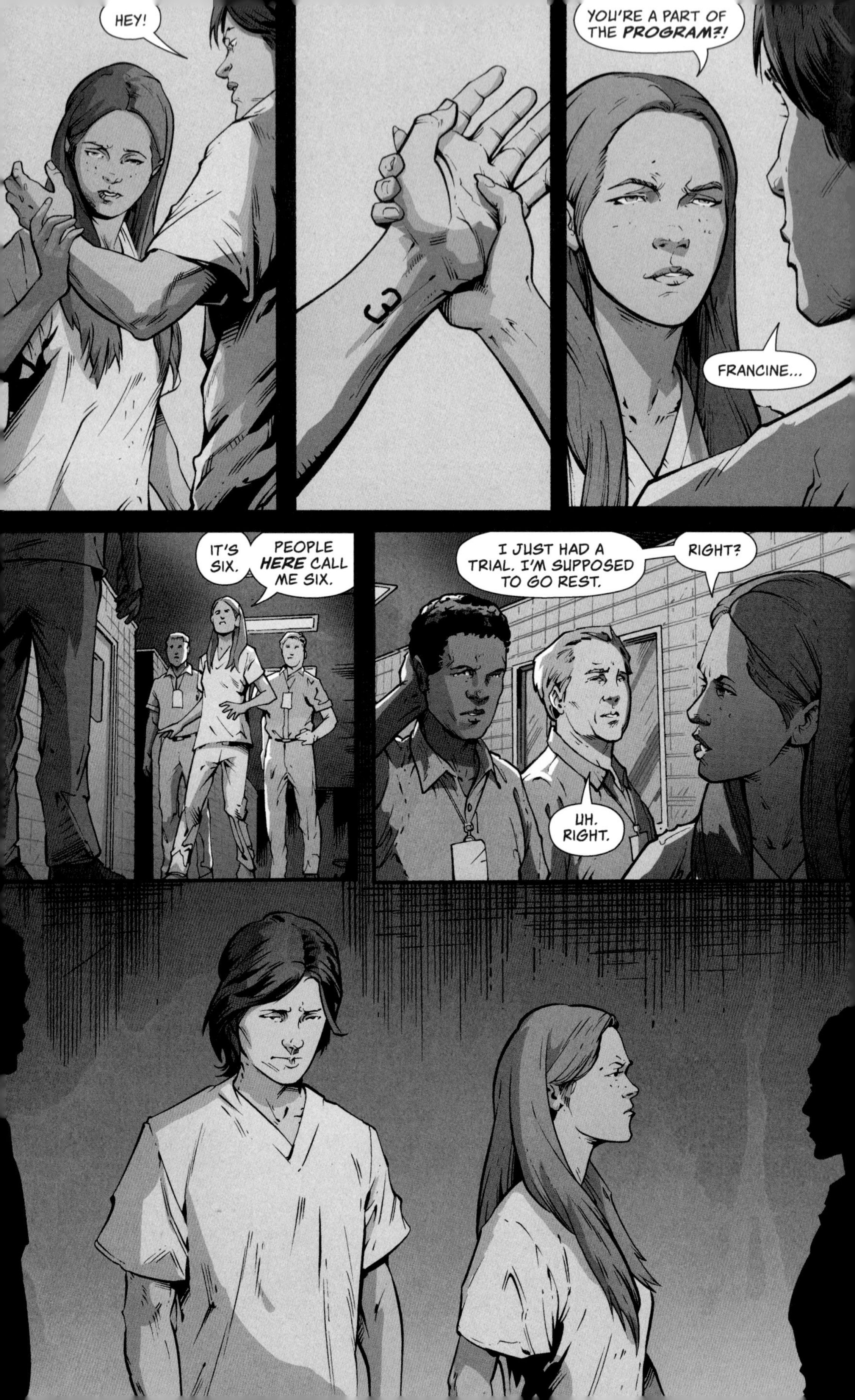
HEY!
YOU'RE A PART OF THE PROGRAM?!
FRANCINE...
IT'S SIX.
PEOPLE HERE CALL ME SIX.
I JUST HAD A TRIAL. I'M SUPPOSED TO GO REST.
RIGHT?
UH. RIGHT.

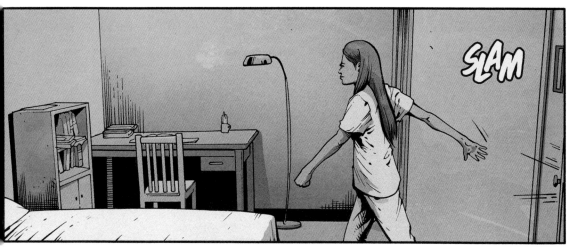

SLAM

HEY. DO YOU, UH--

I'D LIKE TO BE ALONE, PLEASE.

klik

DAMN YOU, RICKY...

THAP

OW...

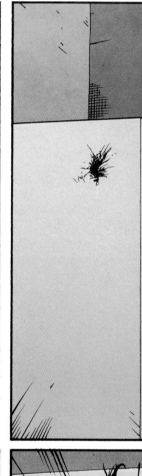

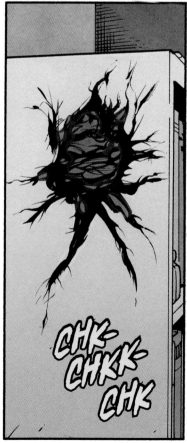

CHK-
CHKK-
CHK

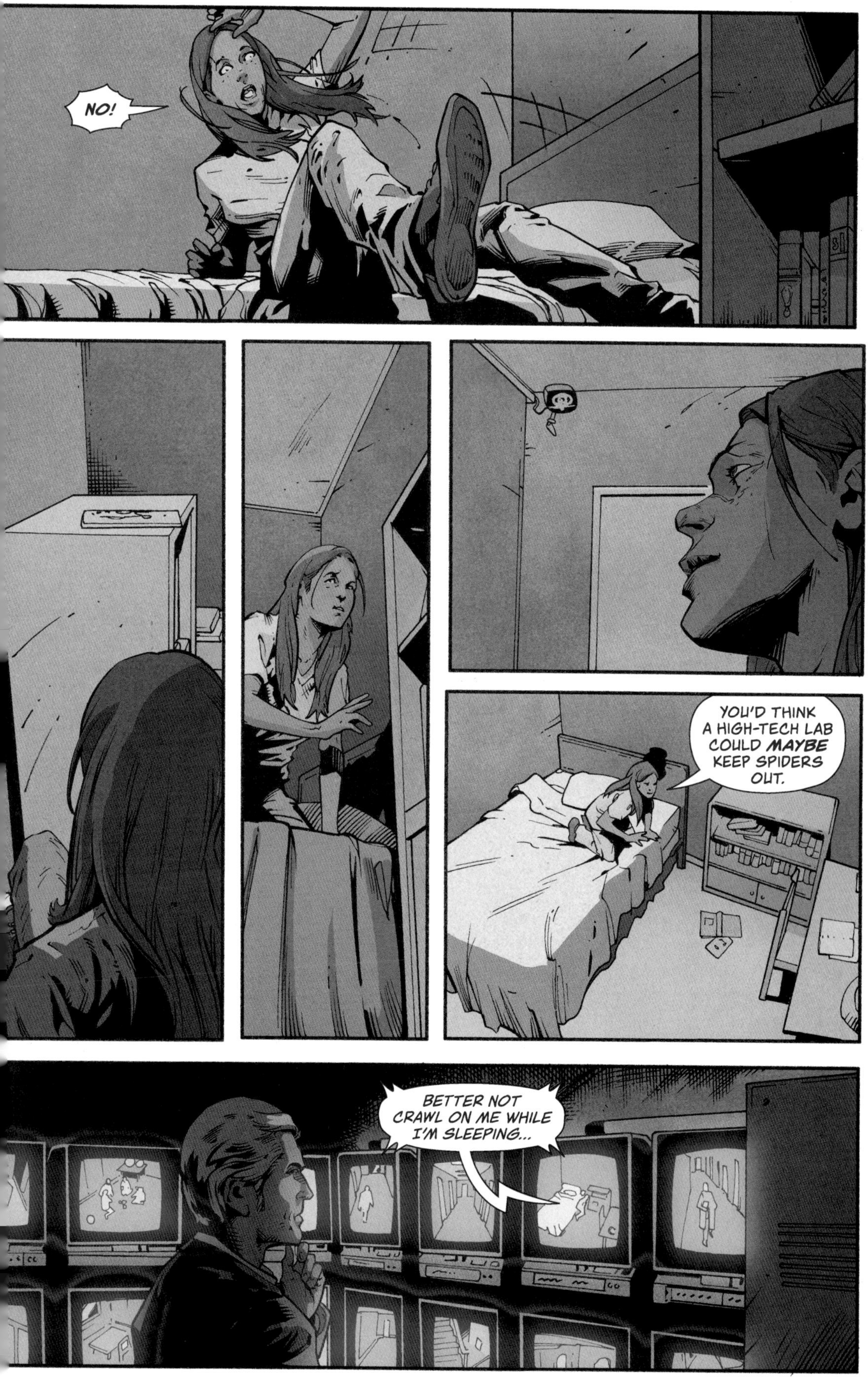
NO!
YOU'D THINK A HIGH-TECH LAB COULD MAYBE KEEP SPIDERS OUT.
BETTER NOT CRAWL ON ME WHILE I'M SLEEPING...

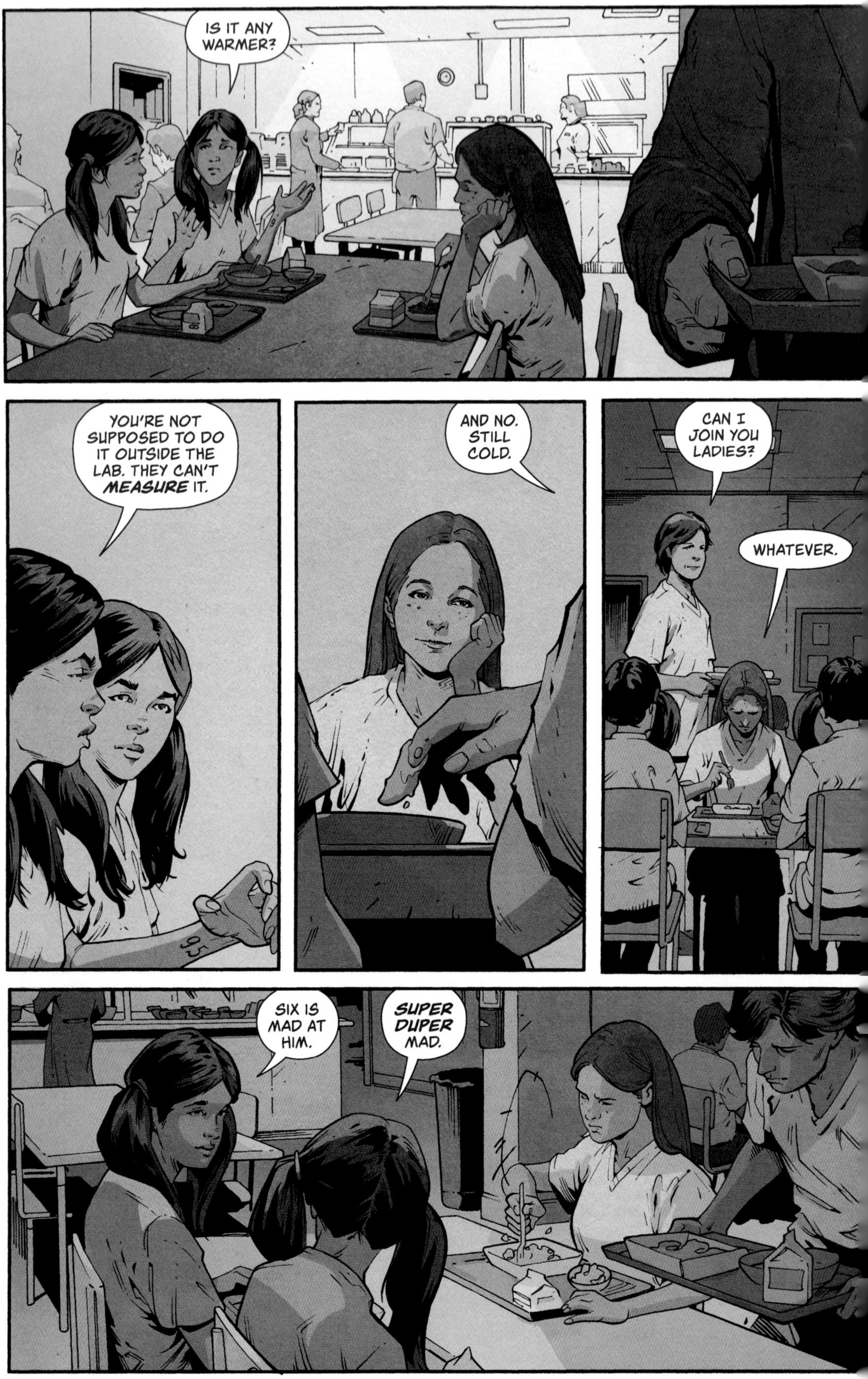
IS IT ANY WARMER?
YOU'RE NOT SUPPOSED TO DO IT OUTSIDE THE LAB. THEY CAN'T *MEASURE* IT.
AND NO. STILL COLD.
CAN I JOIN YOU LADIES?
WHATEVER.
SIX IS MAD AT HIM.
SUPER DUPER MAD.

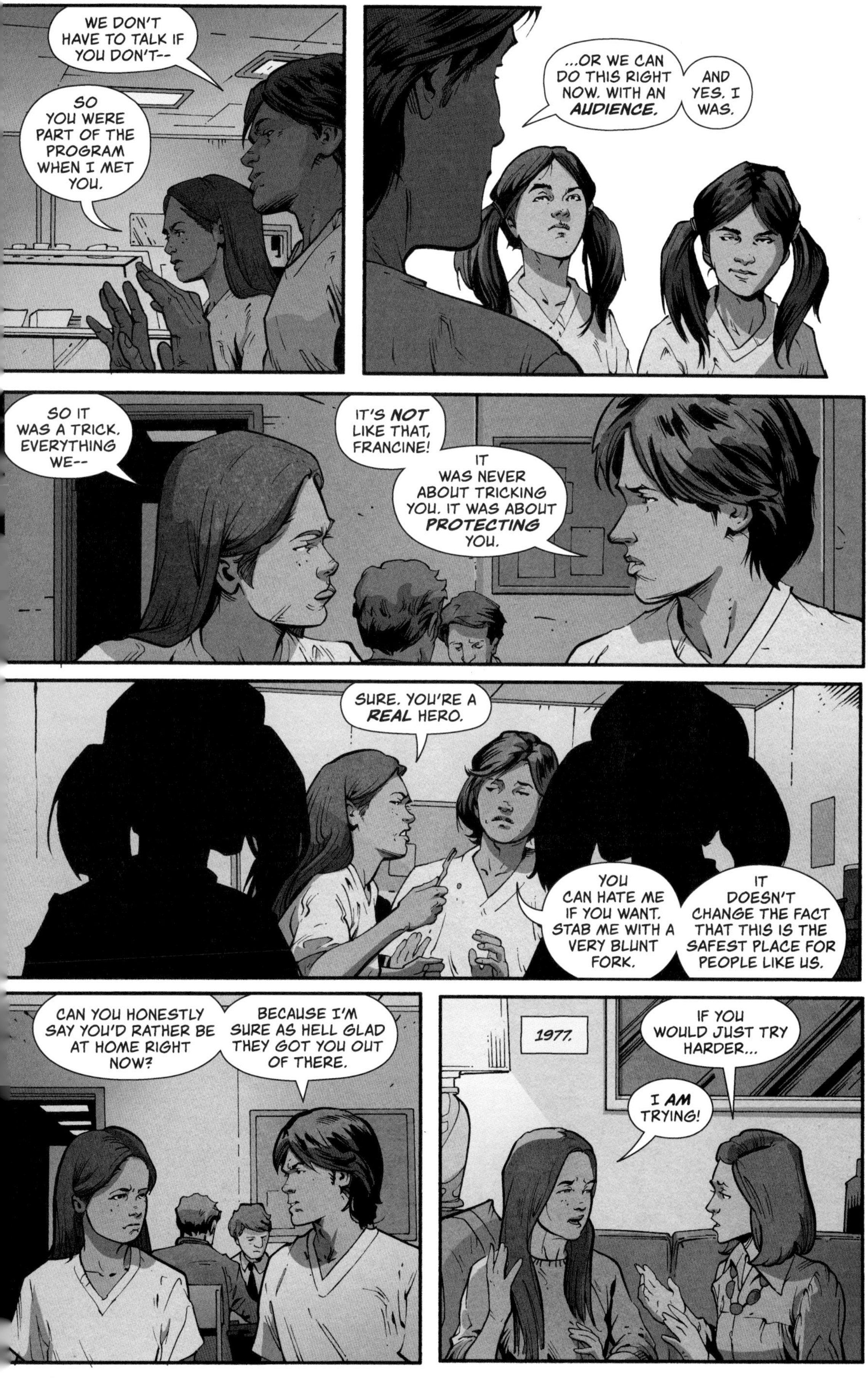
WE DON'T HAVE TO TALK IF YOU DON'T--
SO YOU WERE PART OF THE PROGRAM WHEN I MET YOU.
...OR WE CAN DO THIS RIGHT NOW. WITH AN AUDIENCE.
AND YES. I WAS.
SO IT WAS A TRICK. EVERYTHING WE--
IT'S NOT LIKE THAT, FRANCINE!
IT WAS NEVER ABOUT TRICKING YOU. IT WAS ABOUT PROTECTING YOU.
SURE. YOU'RE A REAL HERO.
YOU CAN HATE ME IF YOU WANT. STAB ME WITH A VERY BLUNT FORK.
IT DOESN'T CHANGE THE FACT THAT THIS IS THE SAFEST PLACE FOR PEOPLE LIKE US.
CAN YOU HONESTLY SAY YOU'D RATHER BE AT HOME RIGHT NOW?
BECAUSE I'M SURE AS HELL GLAD THEY GOT YOU OUT OF THERE.
1977.
IF YOU WOULD JUST TRY HARDER...
I AM TRYING!

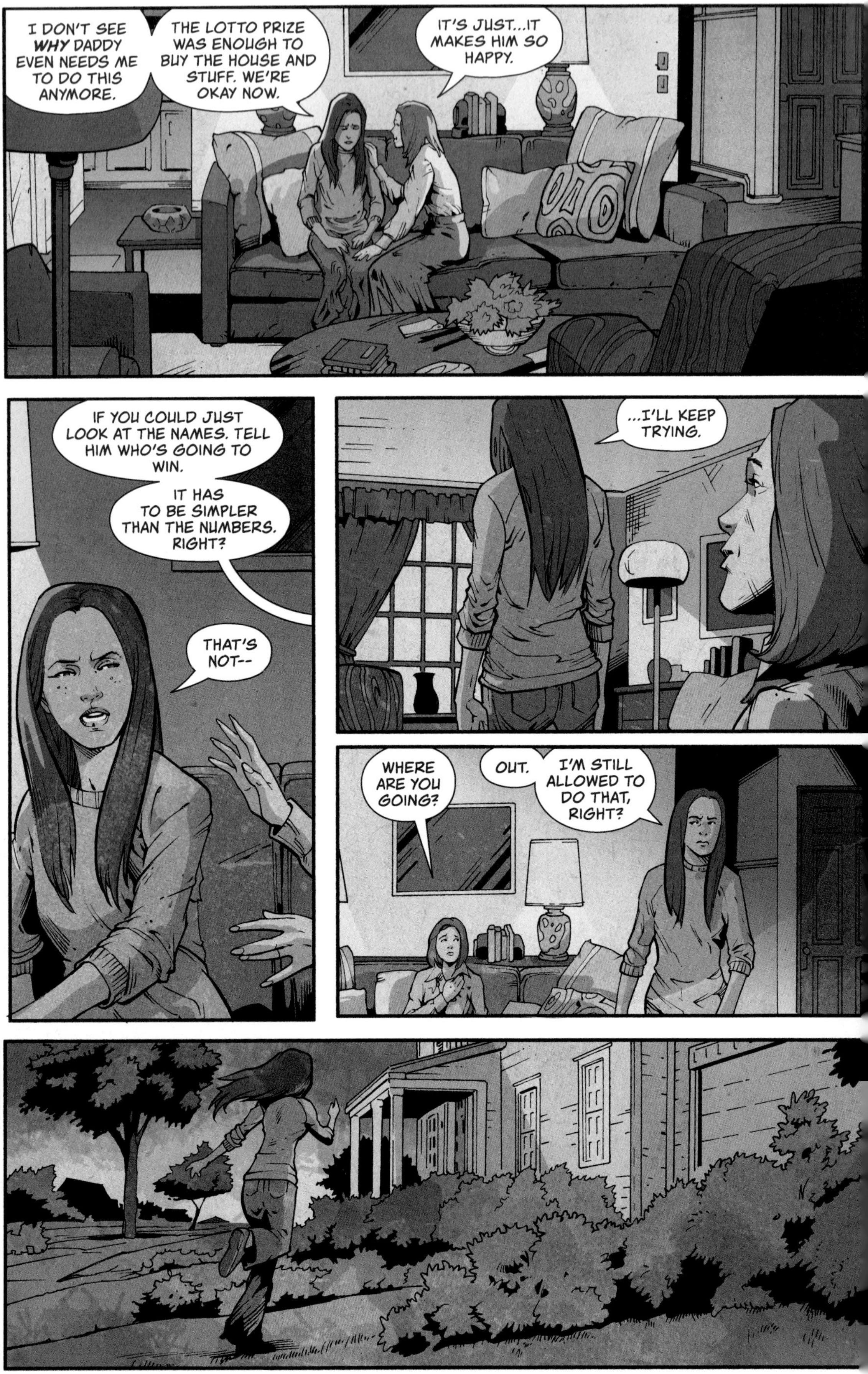
I DON'T SEE *WHY* DADDY EVEN NEEDS ME TO DO THIS ANYMORE.
THE LOTTO PRIZE WAS ENOUGH TO BUY THE HOUSE AND STUFF. WE'RE OKAY NOW.
IT'S JUST...IT MAKES HIM SO HAPPY.
IF YOU COULD JUST LOOK AT THE NAMES. TELL HIM WHO'S GOING TO WIN.
IT HAS TO BE SIMPLER THAN THE NUMBERS. RIGHT?
THAT'S NOT--
...I'LL KEEP TRYING.
WHERE ARE YOU GOING?
OUT.
I'M STILL ALLOWED TO DO THAT, RIGHT?

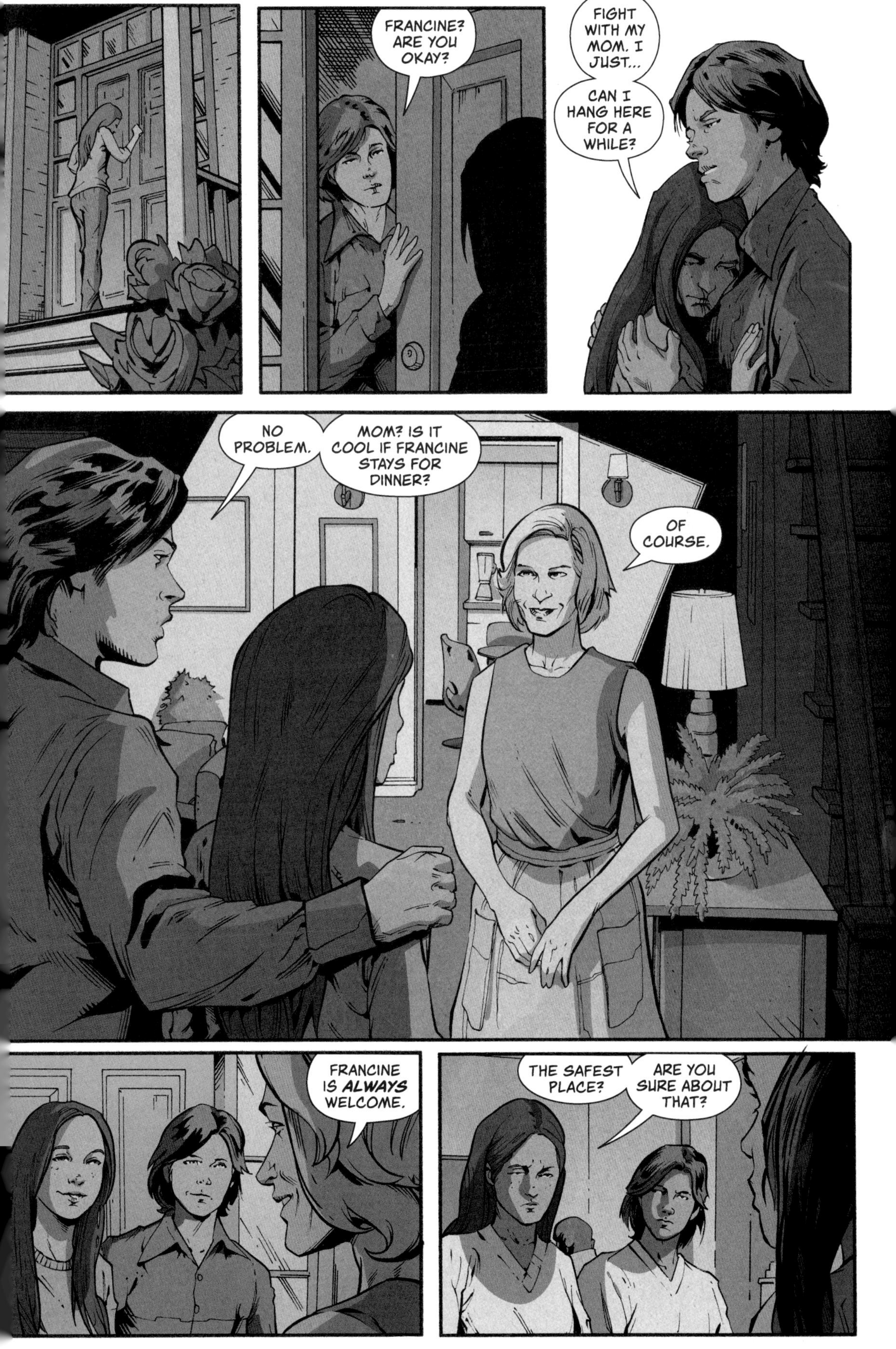
FRANCINE? ARE YOU OKAY?
FIGHT WITH MY MOM. I JUST...
CAN I HANG HERE FOR A WHILE?
NO PROBLEM.
MOM? IS IT COOL IF FRANCINE STAYS FOR DINNER?
OF COURSE.
FRANCINE IS **ALWAYS** WELCOME.
THE SAFEST PLACE?
ARE YOU SURE ABOUT THAT?

WHY WOULDN'T IT BE?

I--

...I WAS JUST ASKING.

YOU'VE BEEN HERE THE LONGEST, RIGHT?

YOU OKAY?

I'M FINE.

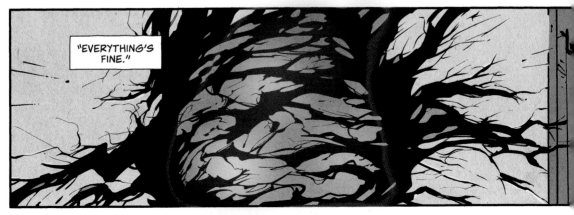

"EVERYTHING'S FINE."

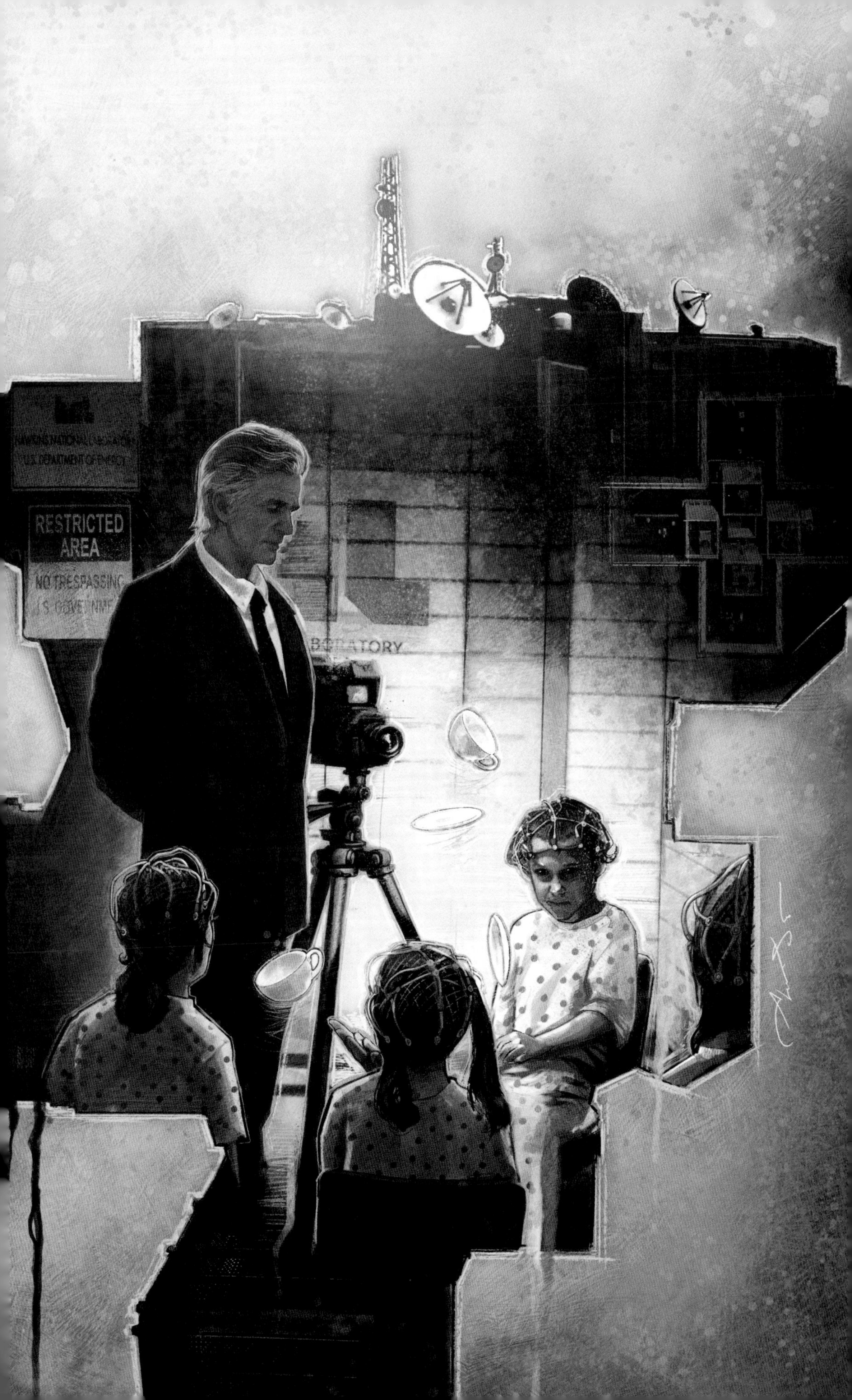

RESTRICTED
AREA
NO TRESPASSING

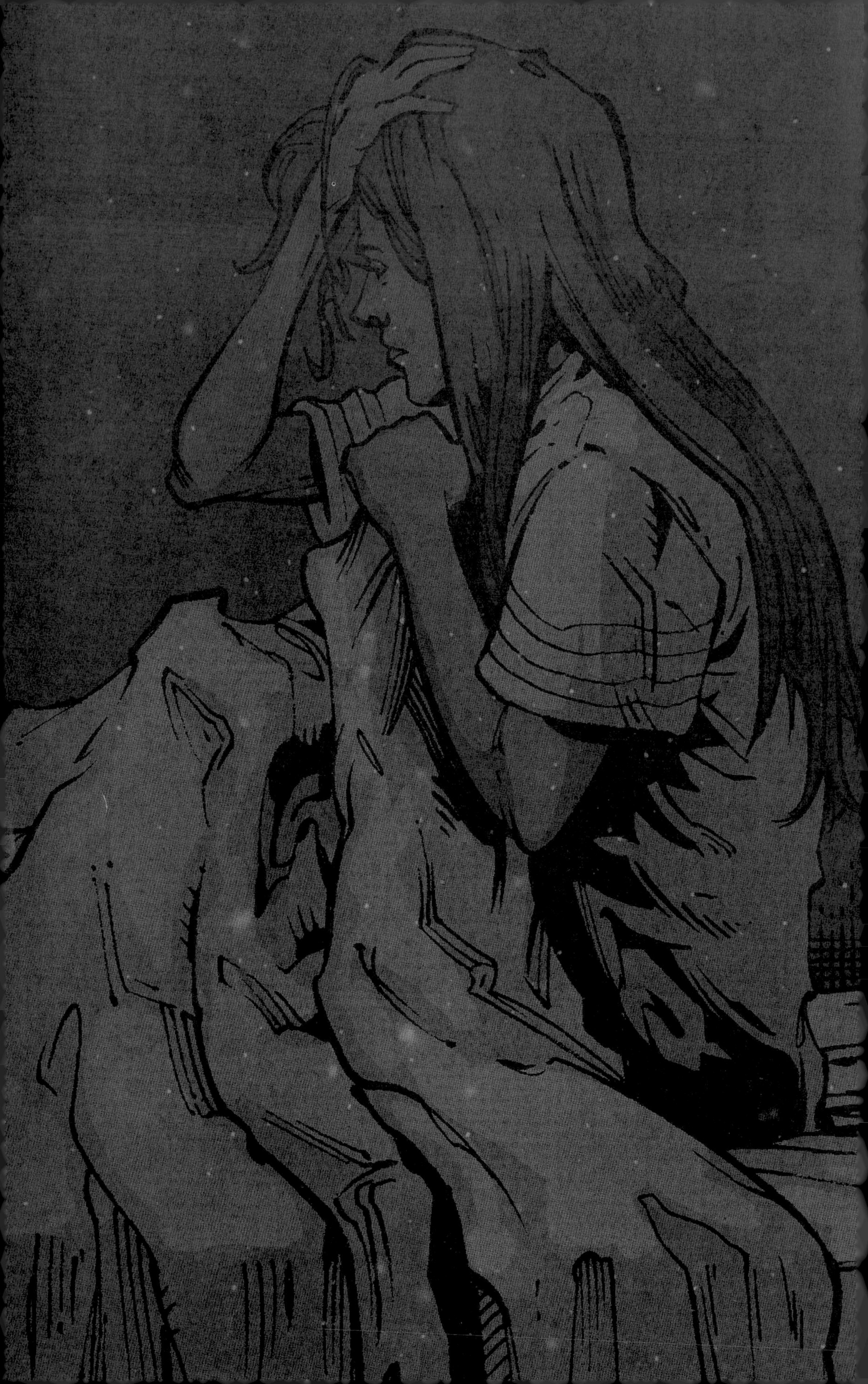

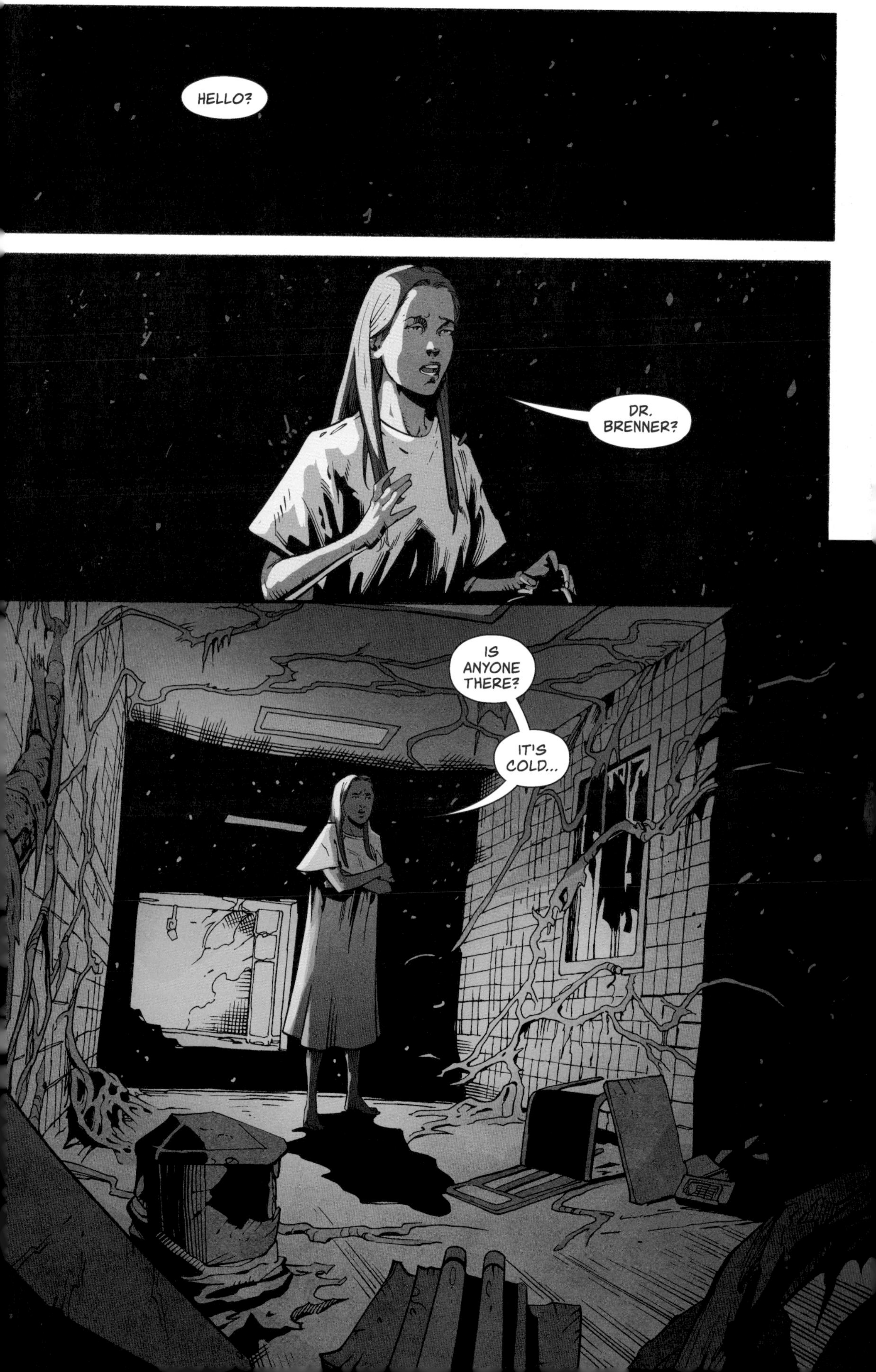
HELLO?
DR. BRENNER?
IS ANYONE THERE?
IT'S COLD...

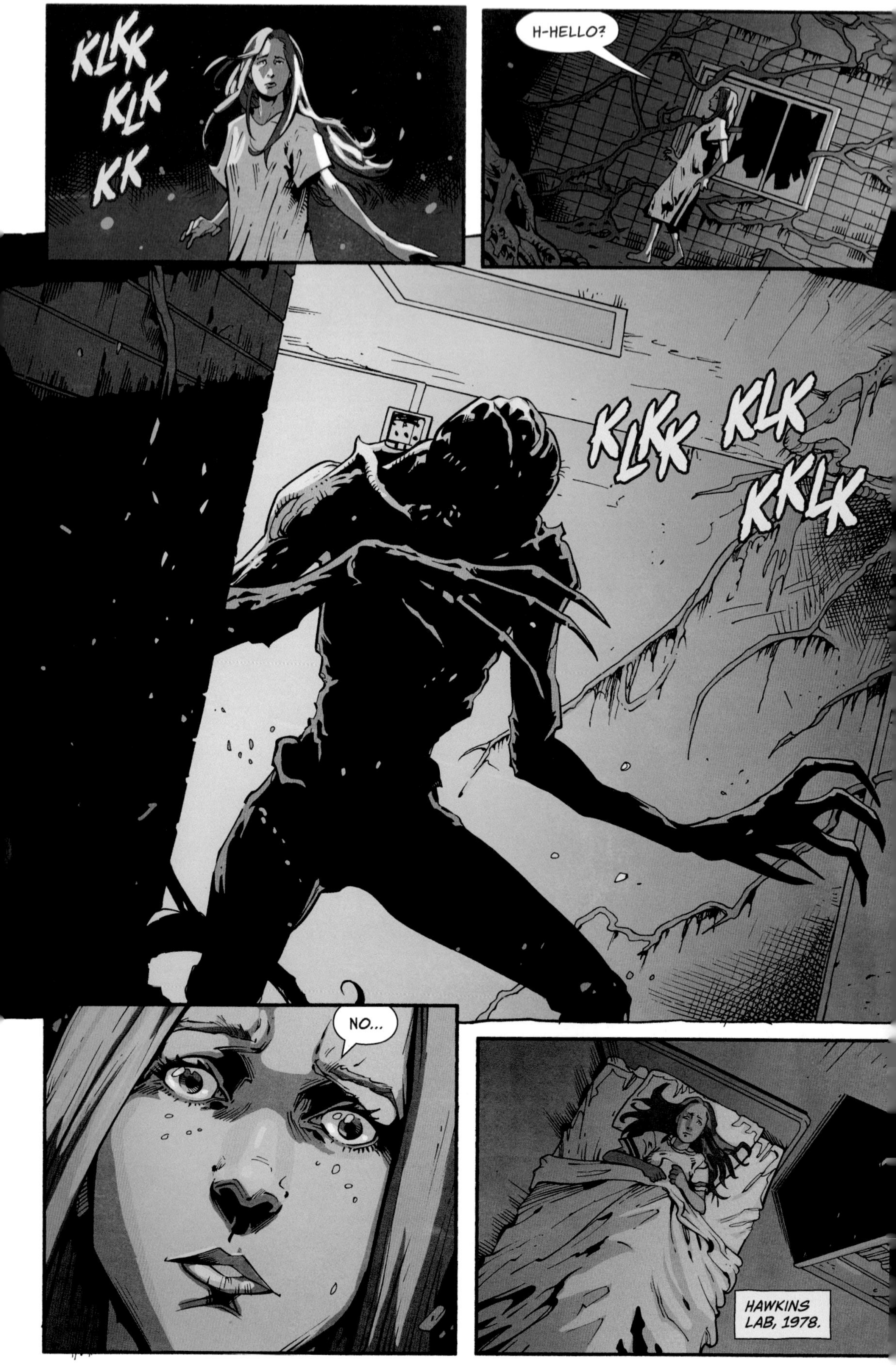
KLKK KLK KK
H-HELLO?
KLKK KLK KKLK
NO...
HAWKINS LAB, 1978.

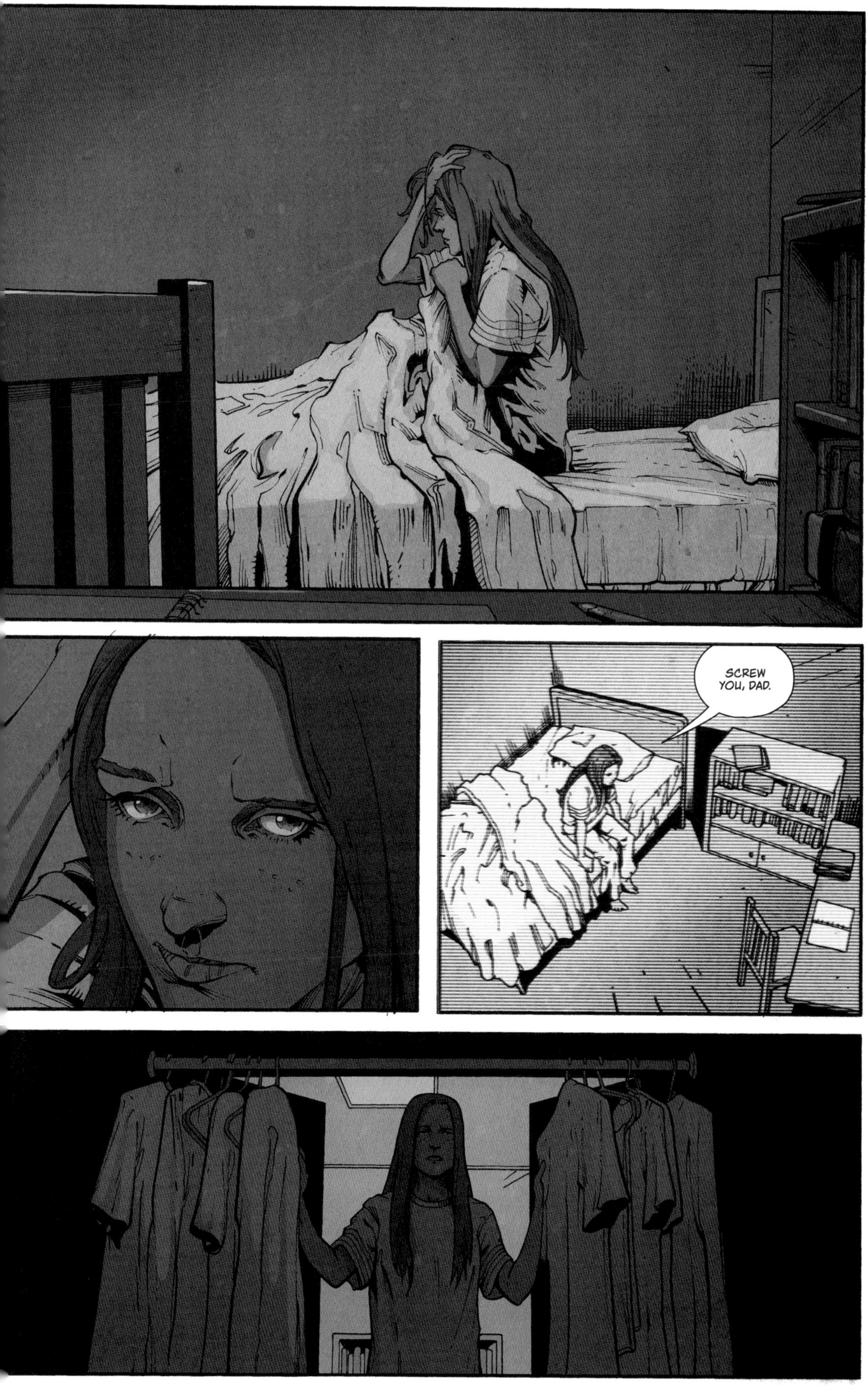
SCREW YOU, DAD.

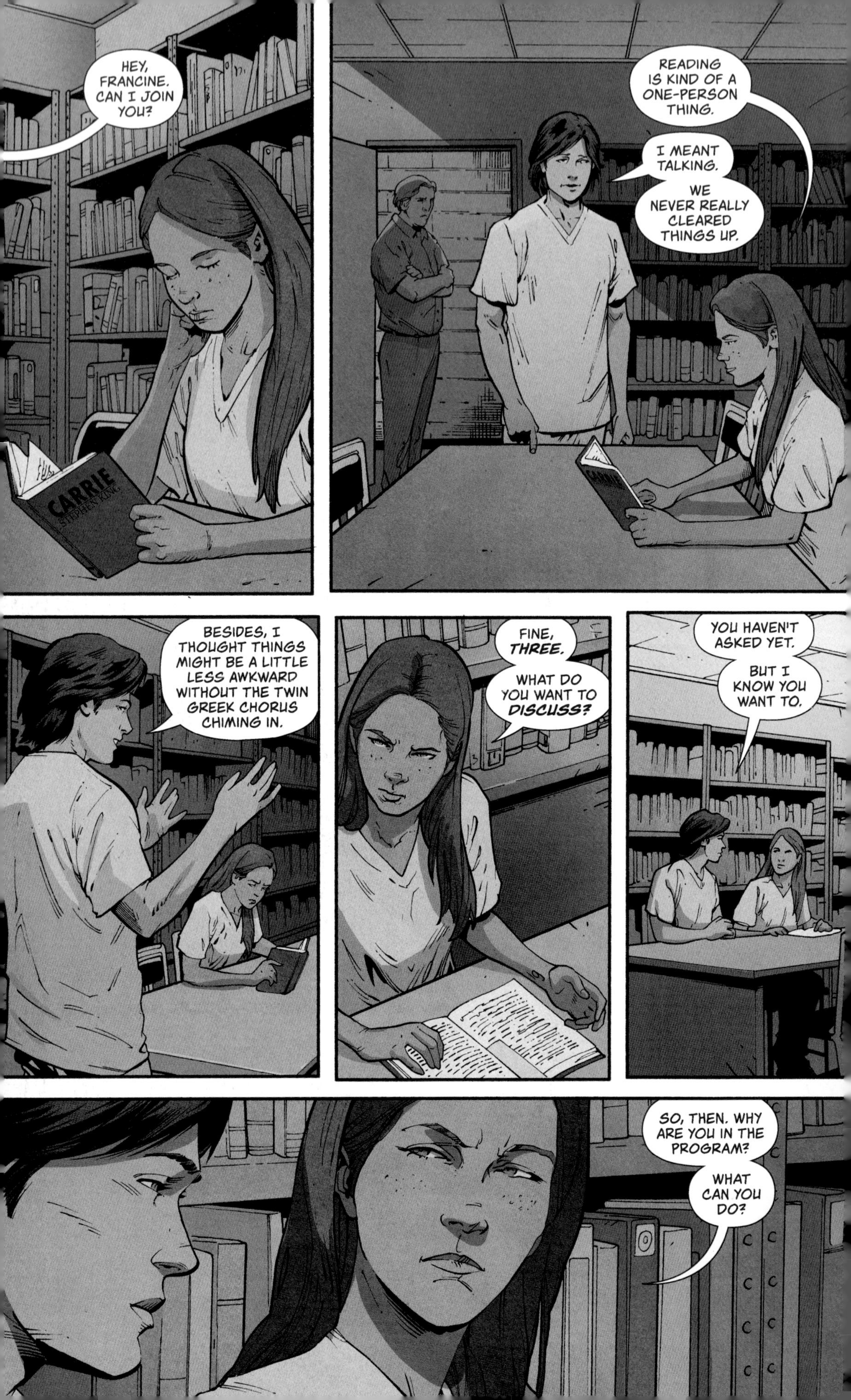
HEY, FRANCINE. CAN I JOIN YOU?
CARRIE
STEPHEN KING
READING IS KIND OF A ONE-PERSON THING.
I MEANT TALKING.
WE NEVER REALLY CLEARED THINGS UP.
BESIDES, I THOUGHT THINGS MIGHT BE A LITTLE LESS AWKWARD WITHOUT THE TWIN GREEK CHORUS CHIMING IN.
FINE, THREE.
WHAT DO YOU WANT TO DISCUSS?
YOU HAVEN'T ASKED YET.
BUT I KNOW YOU WANT TO.
SO, THEN. WHY ARE YOU IN THE PROGRAM?
WHAT CAN YOU DO?

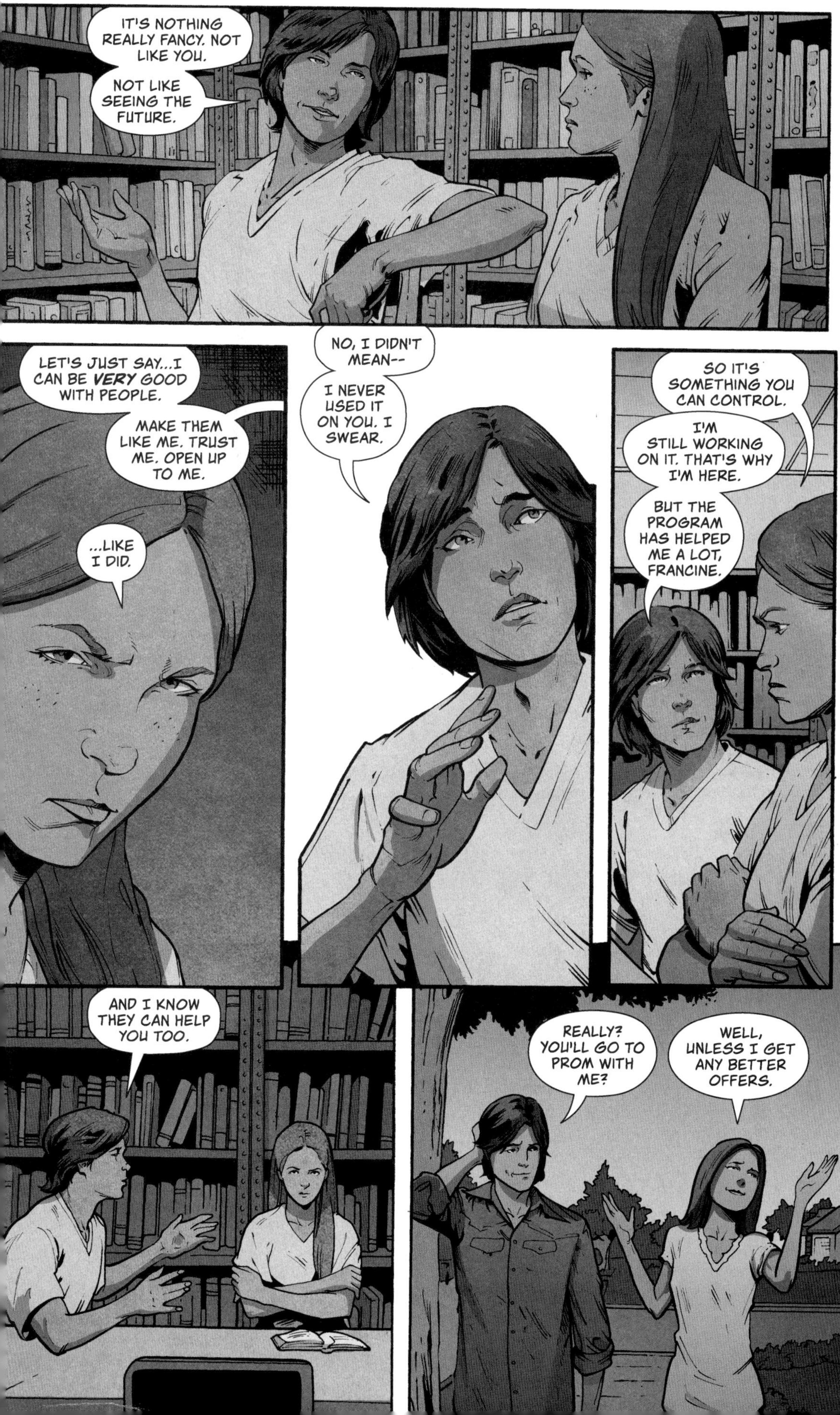
IT'S NOTHING REALLY FANCY. NOT LIKE YOU.
NOT LIKE SEEING THE FUTURE.
LET'S JUST SAY...I CAN BE *VERY* GOOD WITH PEOPLE.
MAKE THEM LIKE ME. TRUST ME. OPEN UP TO ME.
...LIKE I DID.
NO, I DIDN'T MEAN--
I NEVER USED IT ON YOU. I SWEAR.
SO IT'S SOMETHING YOU CAN CONTROL.
I'M STILL WORKING ON IT. THAT'S WHY I'M HERE.
BUT THE PROGRAM HAS HELPED ME A LOT, FRANCINE.
AND I KNOW THEY CAN HELP YOU TOO.
REALLY? YOU'LL GO TO PROM WITH ME?
WELL, UNLESS I GET ANY BETTER OFFERS.

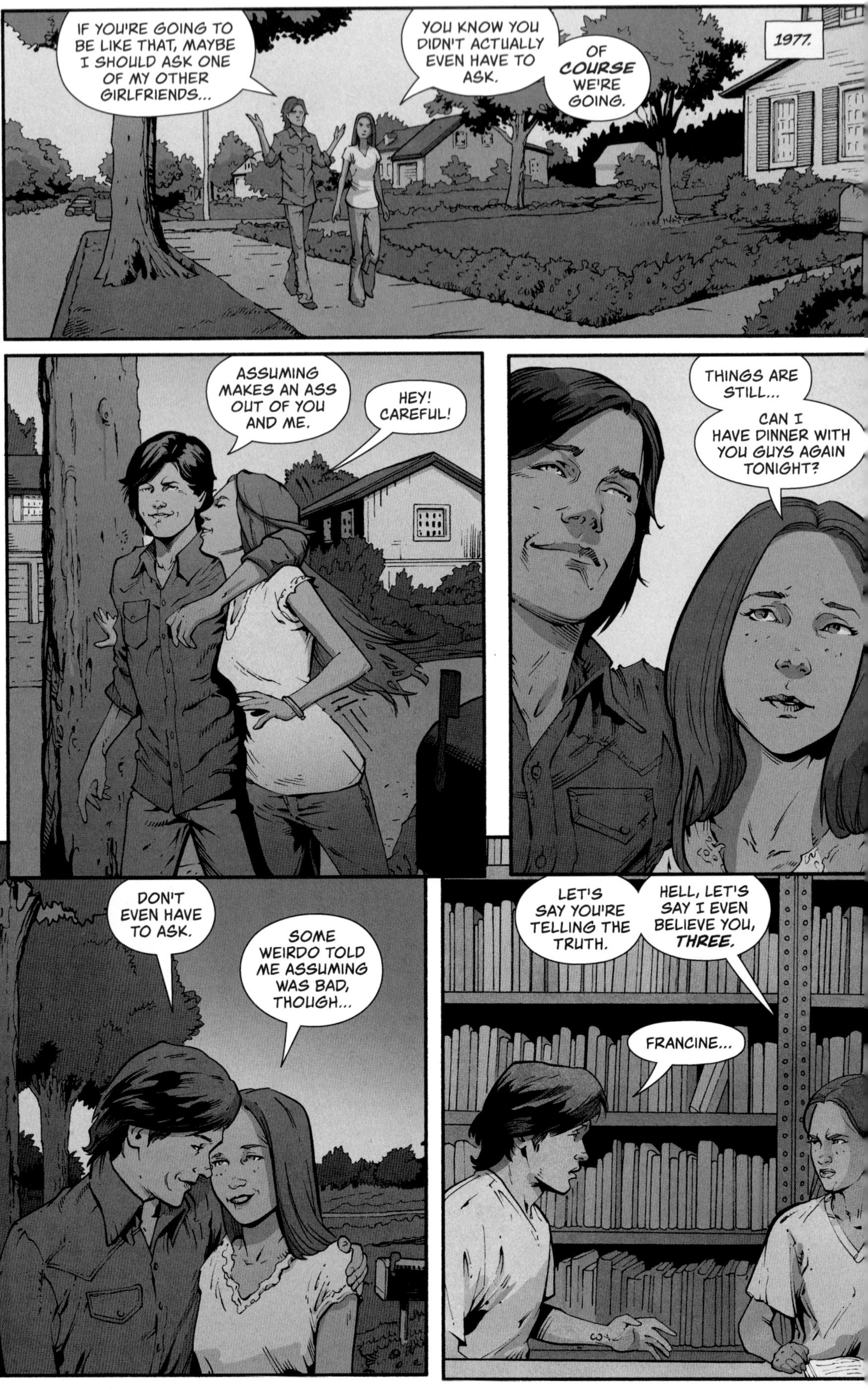
1977.
IF YOU'RE GOING TO BE LIKE THAT, MAYBE I SHOULD ASK ONE OF MY OTHER GIRLFRIENDS...
YOU KNOW YOU DIDN'T ACTUALLY EVEN HAVE TO ASK.
OF COURSE WE'RE GOING.
ASSUMING MAKES AN ASS OUT OF YOU AND ME.
HEY! CAREFUL!
THINGS ARE STILL...
CAN I HAVE DINNER WITH YOU GUYS AGAIN TONIGHT?
DON'T EVEN HAVE TO ASK.
SOME WEIRDO TOLD ME ASSUMING WAS BAD, THOUGH...
LET'S SAY YOU'RE TELLING THE TRUTH.
HELL, LET'S SAY I EVEN BELIEVE YOU, THREE.
FRANCINE...

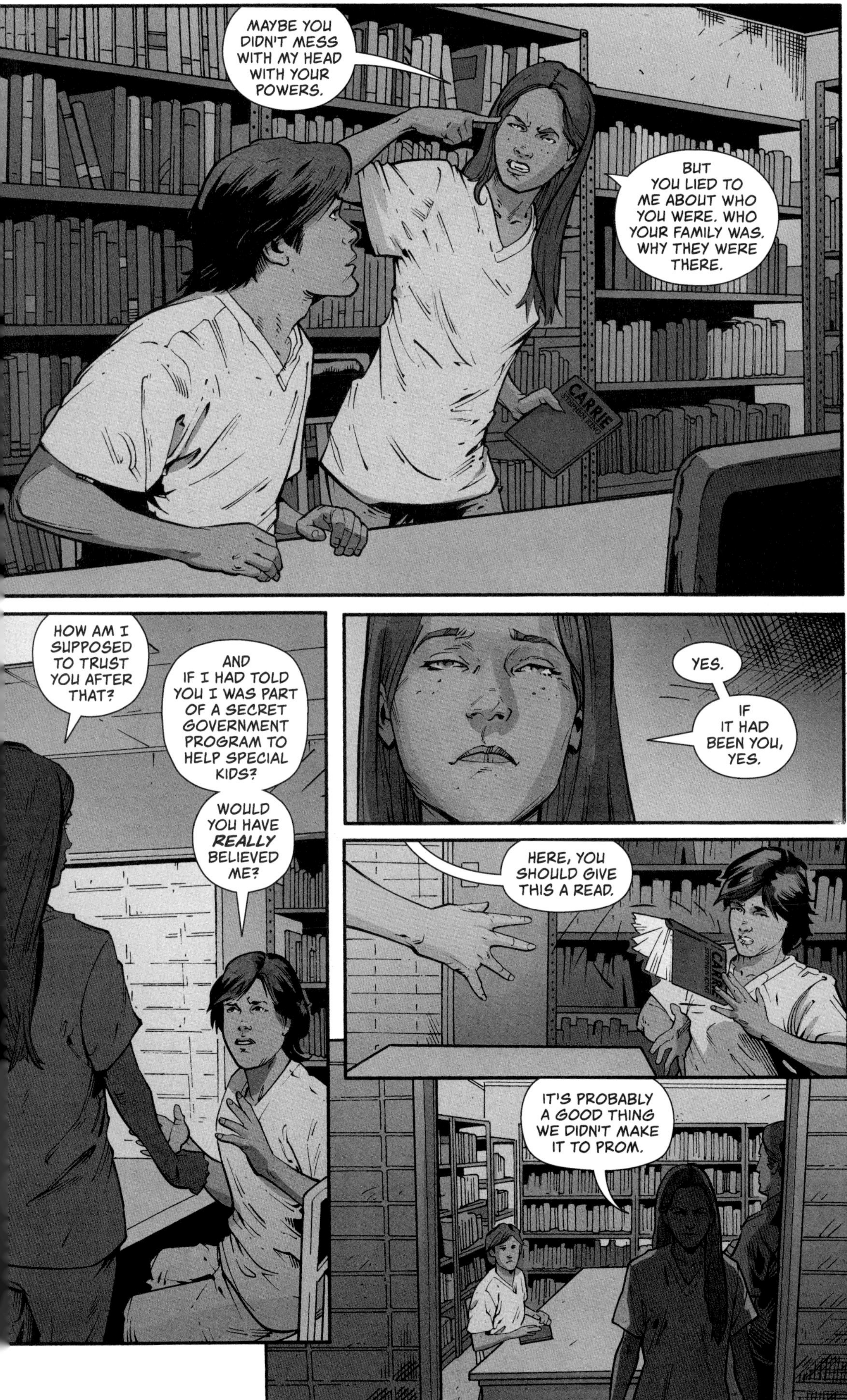

MAYBE YOU DIDN'T MESS WITH MY HEAD WITH YOUR POWERS.
BUT YOU LIED TO ME ABOUT WHO YOU WERE. WHO YOUR FAMILY WAS. WHY THEY WERE THERE.
CARRIE
STEPHEN KING
HOW AM I SUPPOSED TO TRUST YOU AFTER THAT?
AND IF I HAD TOLD YOU I WAS PART OF A SECRET GOVERNMENT PROGRAM TO HELP SPECIAL KIDS?
WOULD YOU HAVE *REALLY* BELIEVED ME?
YES.
IF IT HAD BEEN YOU, YES.
HERE, YOU SHOULD GIVE THIS A READ.
IT'S PROBABLY A GOOD THING WE DIDN'T MAKE IT TO PROM.

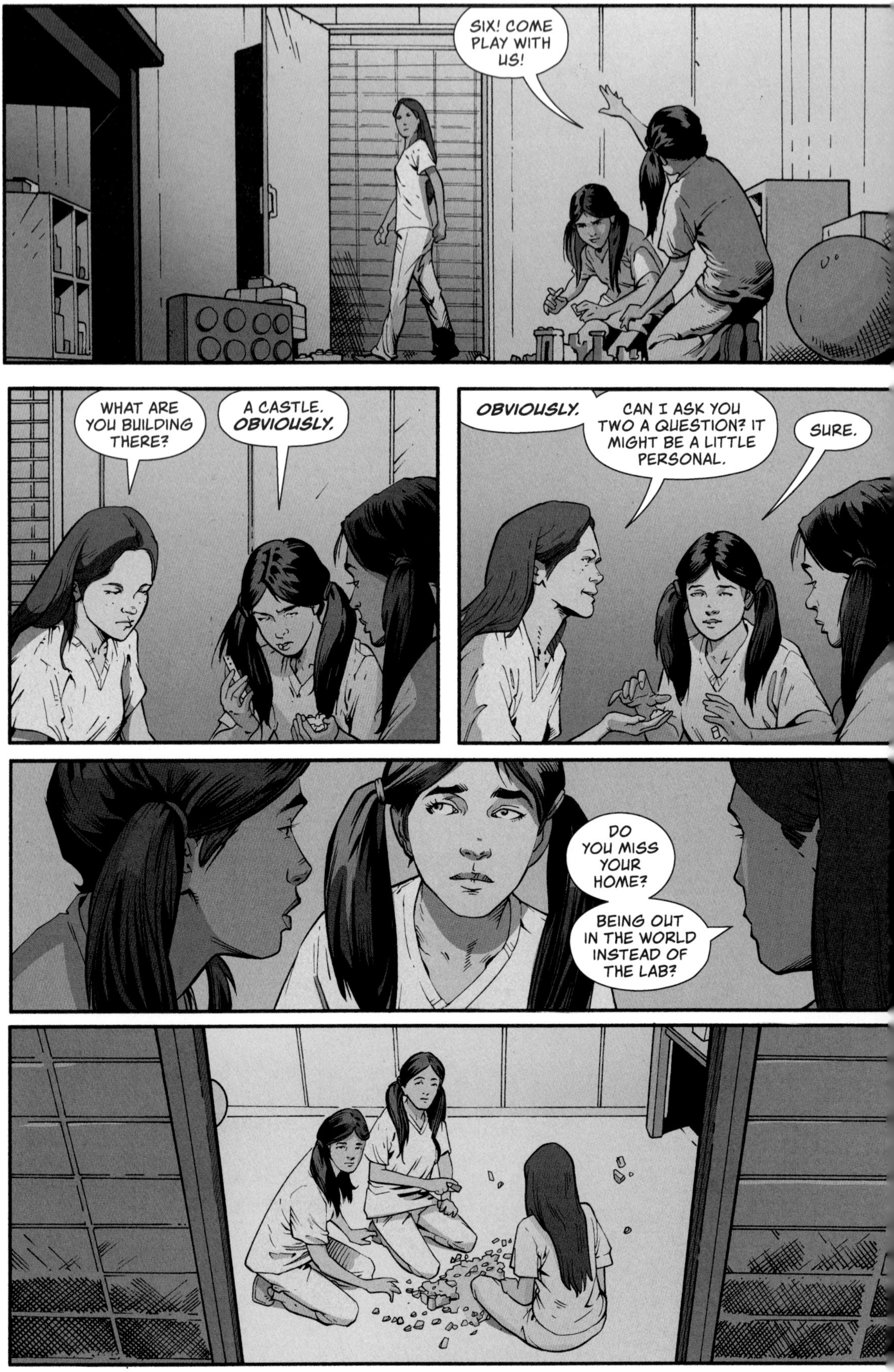
SIX! COME PLAY WITH US!
WHAT ARE YOU BUILDING THERE?
A CASTLE. OBVIOUSLY.
OBVIOUSLY.
CAN I ASK YOU TWO A QUESTION? IT MIGHT BE A LITTLE PERSONAL.
SURE.
DO YOU MISS YOUR HOME?
BEING OUT IN THE WORLD INSTEAD OF THE LAB?

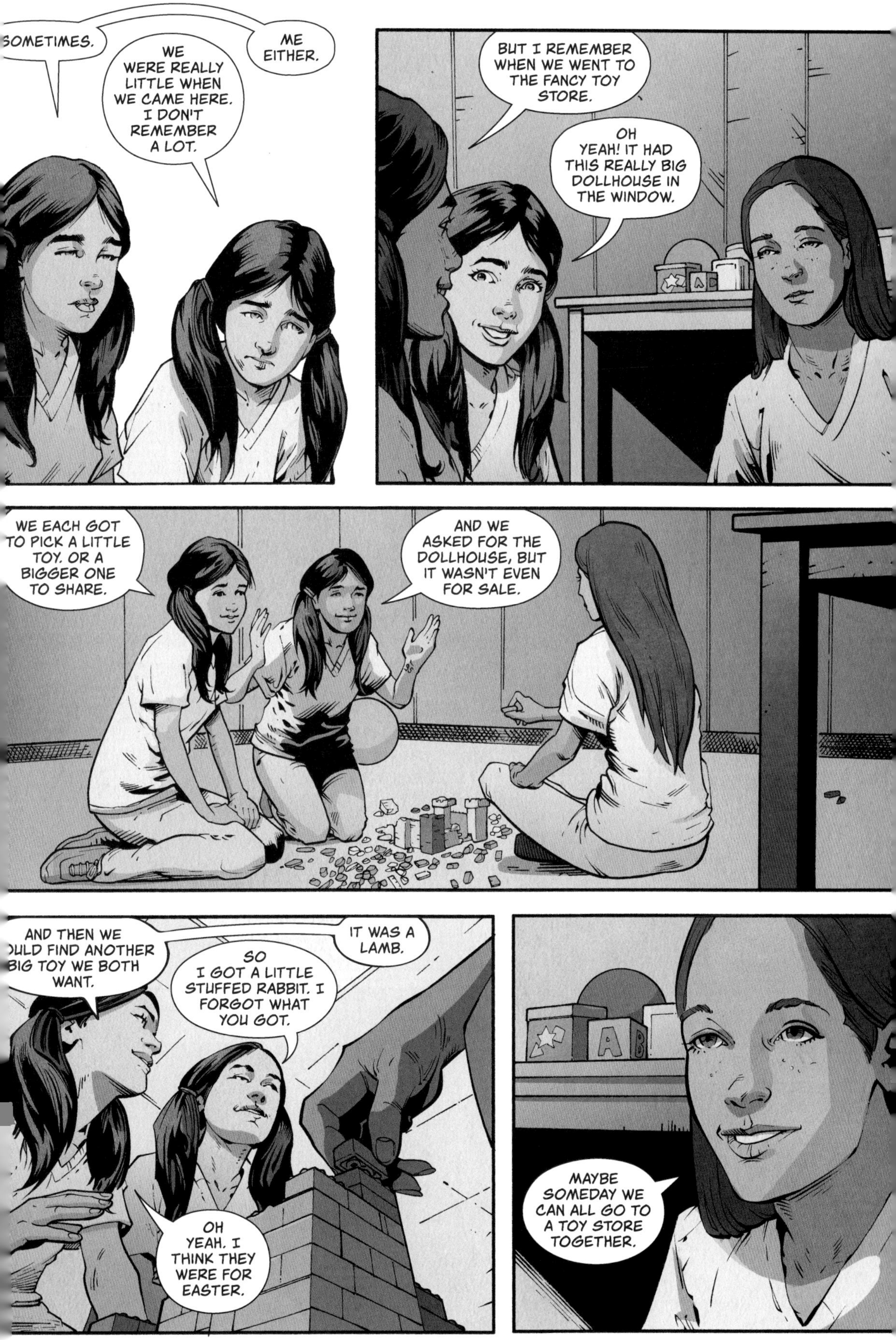
SOMETIMES.
WE WERE REALLY LITTLE WHEN WE CAME HERE. I DON'T REMEMBER A LOT.
ME EITHER.
BUT I REMEMBER WHEN WE WENT TO THE FANCY TOY STORE.
OH YEAH! IT HAD THIS REALLY BIG DOLLHOUSE IN THE WINDOW.
WE EACH GOT TO PICK A LITTLE TOY. OR A BIGGER ONE TO SHARE.
AND WE ASKED FOR THE DOLLHOUSE, BUT IT WASN'T EVEN FOR SALE.
AND THEN WE OULD FIND ANOTHER BIG TOY WE BOTH WANT.
SO I GOT A LITTLE STUFFED RABBIT. I FORGOT WHAT YOU GOT.
IT WAS A LAMB.
OH YEAH. I THINK THEY WERE FOR EASTER.
MAYBE SOMEDAY WE CAN ALL GO TO A TOY STORE TOGETHER.

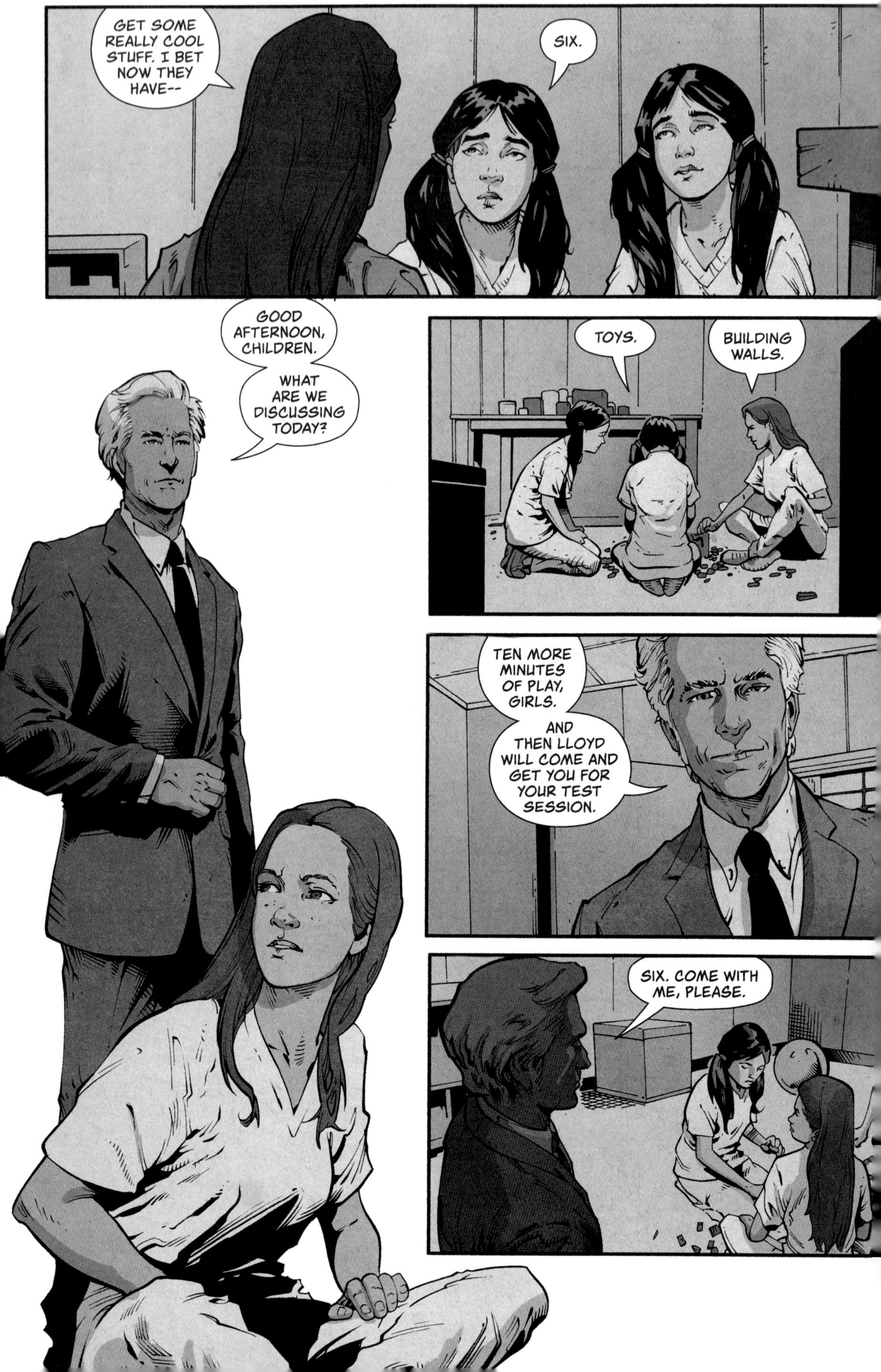
GET SOME REALLY COOL STUFF. I BET NOW THEY HAVE--
SIX.
GOOD AFTERNOON, CHILDREN.
WHAT ARE WE DISCUSSING TODAY?
TOYS.
BUILDING WALLS.
TEN MORE MINUTES OF PLAY, GIRLS.
AND THEN LLOYD WILL COME AND GET YOU FOR YOUR TEST SESSION.
SIX. COME WITH ME, PLEASE.

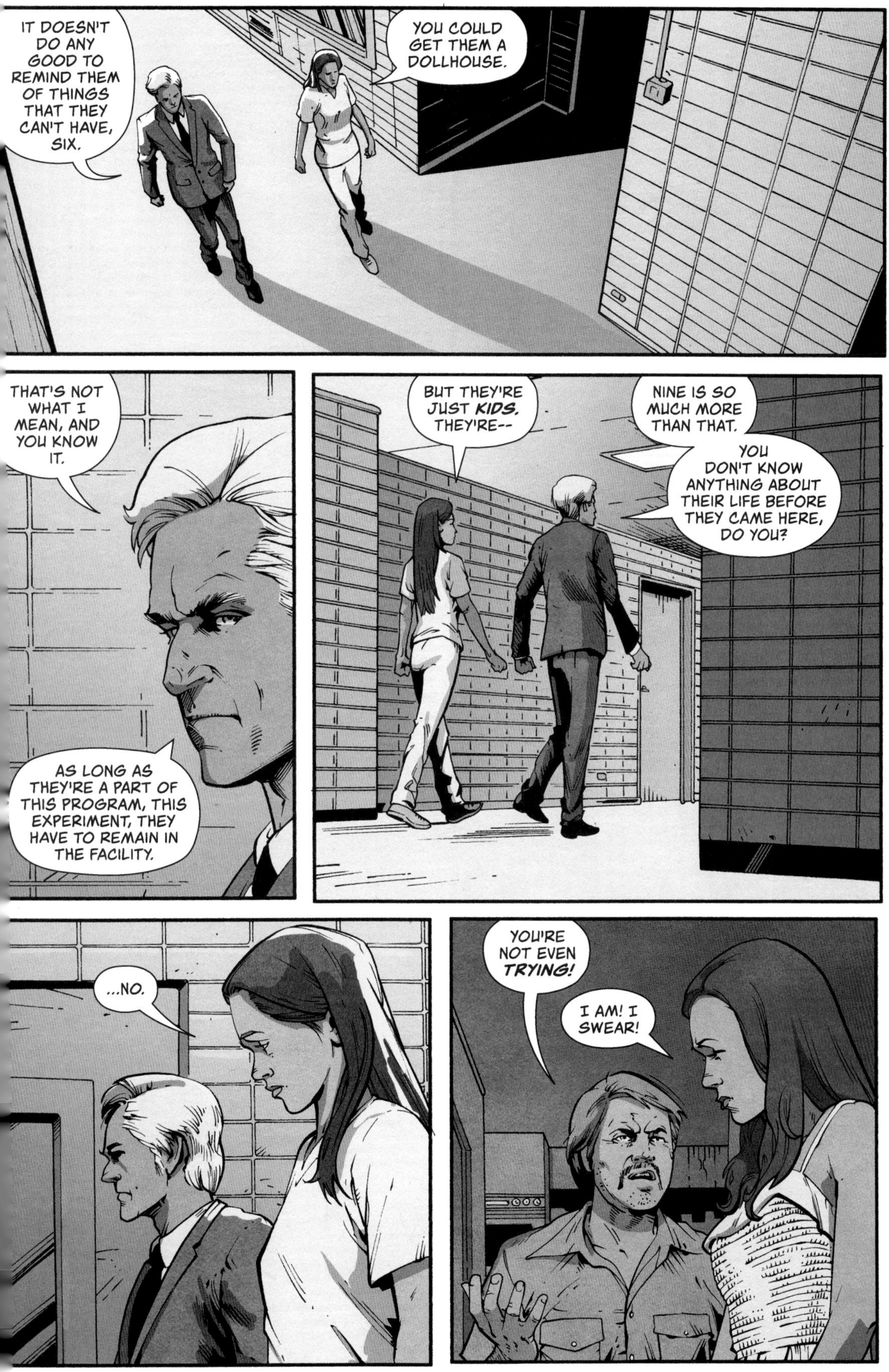
IT DOESN'T DO ANY GOOD TO REMIND THEM OF THINGS THAT THEY CAN'T HAVE, SIX.
YOU COULD GET THEM A DOLLHOUSE.
THAT'S NOT WHAT I MEAN, AND YOU KNOW IT.
AS LONG AS THEY'RE A PART OF THIS PROGRAM, THIS EXPERIMENT, THEY HAVE TO REMAIN IN THE FACILITY.
BUT THEY'RE JUST *KIDS.* THEY'RE--
NINE IS SO MUCH MORE THAN THAT.
YOU DON'T KNOW ANYTHING ABOUT THEIR LIFE BEFORE THEY CAME HERE, DO YOU?
...NO.
YOU'RE NOT EVEN *TRYING!*
I AM! I SWEAR!

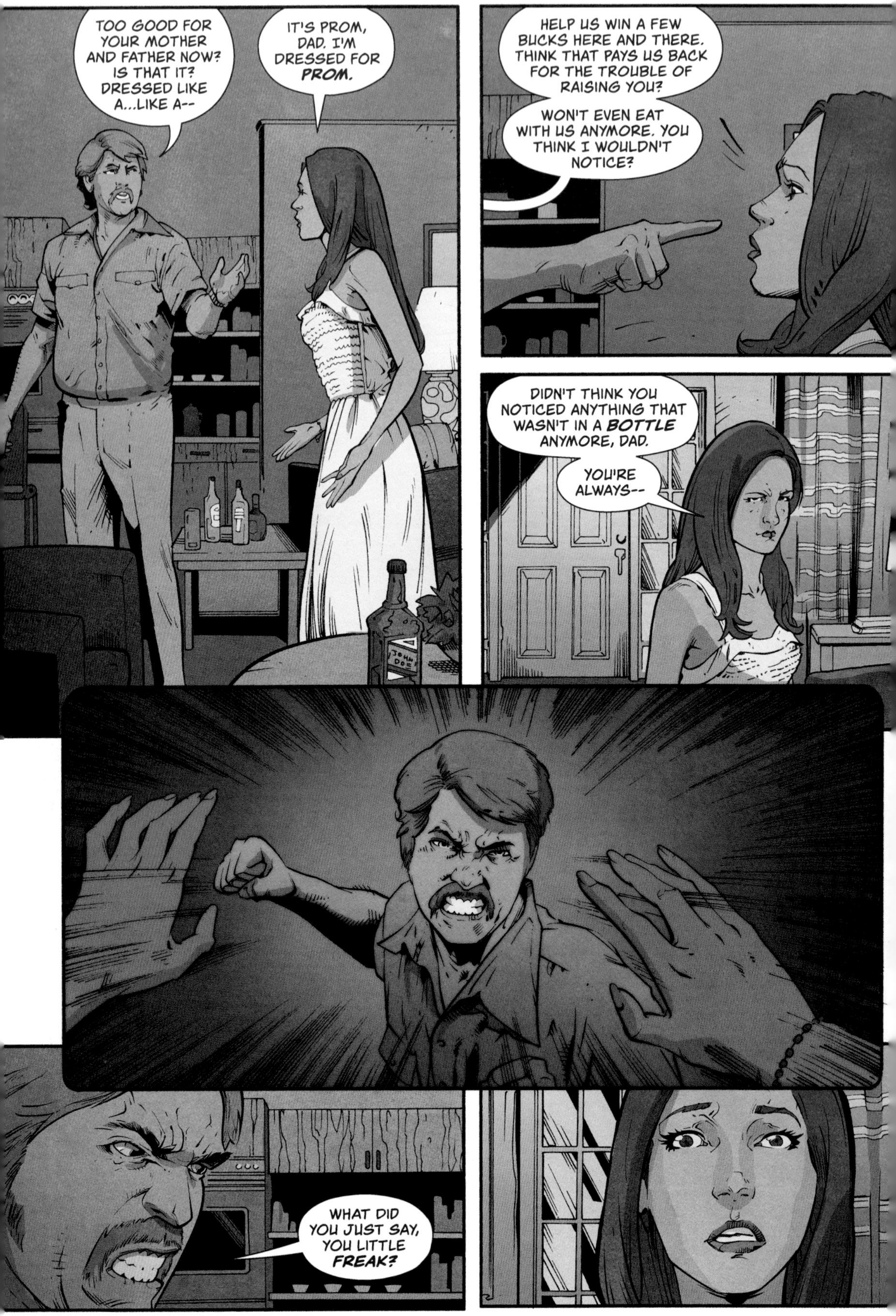
TOO GOOD FOR YOUR MOTHER AND FATHER NOW? IS THAT IT? DRESSED LIKE A...LIKE A--
IT'S PROM, DAD. I'M DRESSED FOR **PROM.**
HELP US WIN A FEW BUCKS HERE AND THERE. THINK THAT PAYS US BACK FOR THE TROUBLE OF RAISING YOU?
WON'T EVEN EAT WITH US ANYMORE. YOU THINK I WOULDN'T NOTICE?
DIDN'T THINK YOU NOTICED ANYTHING THAT WASN'T IN A **BOTTLE** ANYMORE, DAD.
YOU'RE ALWAYS--
WHAT DID YOU JUST SAY, YOU LITTLE **FREAK?**

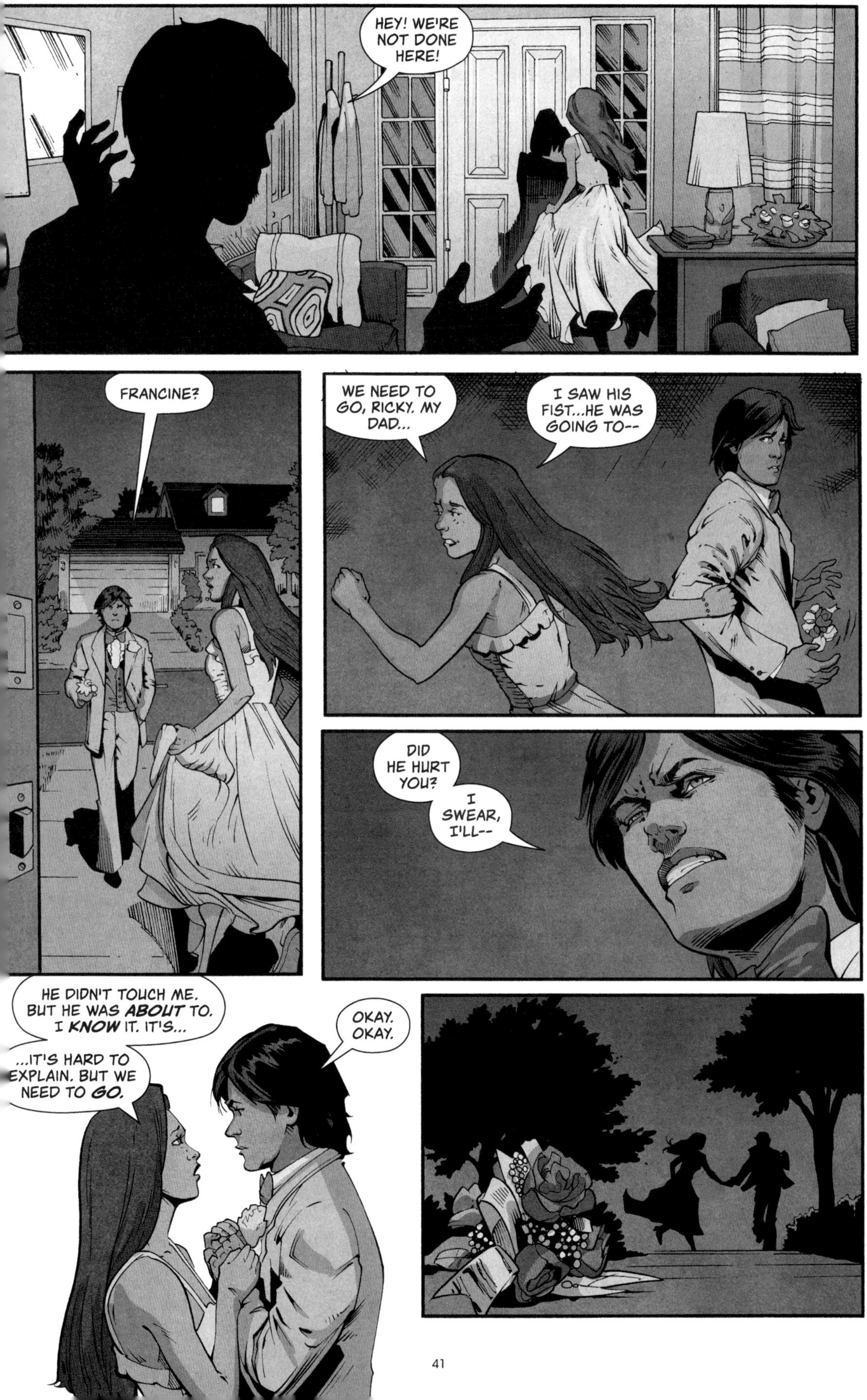
HEY! WE'RE NOT DONE HERE!
FRANCINE?
WE NEED TO GO, RICKY. MY DAD...
I SAW HIS FIST...HE WAS GOING TO--
DID HE HURT YOU?
I SWEAR, I'LL--
HE DIDN'T TOUCH ME. BUT HE WAS ABOUT TO. I KNOW IT. IT'S...
...IT'S HARD TO EXPLAIN. BUT WE NEED TO GO.
OKAY. OKAY.

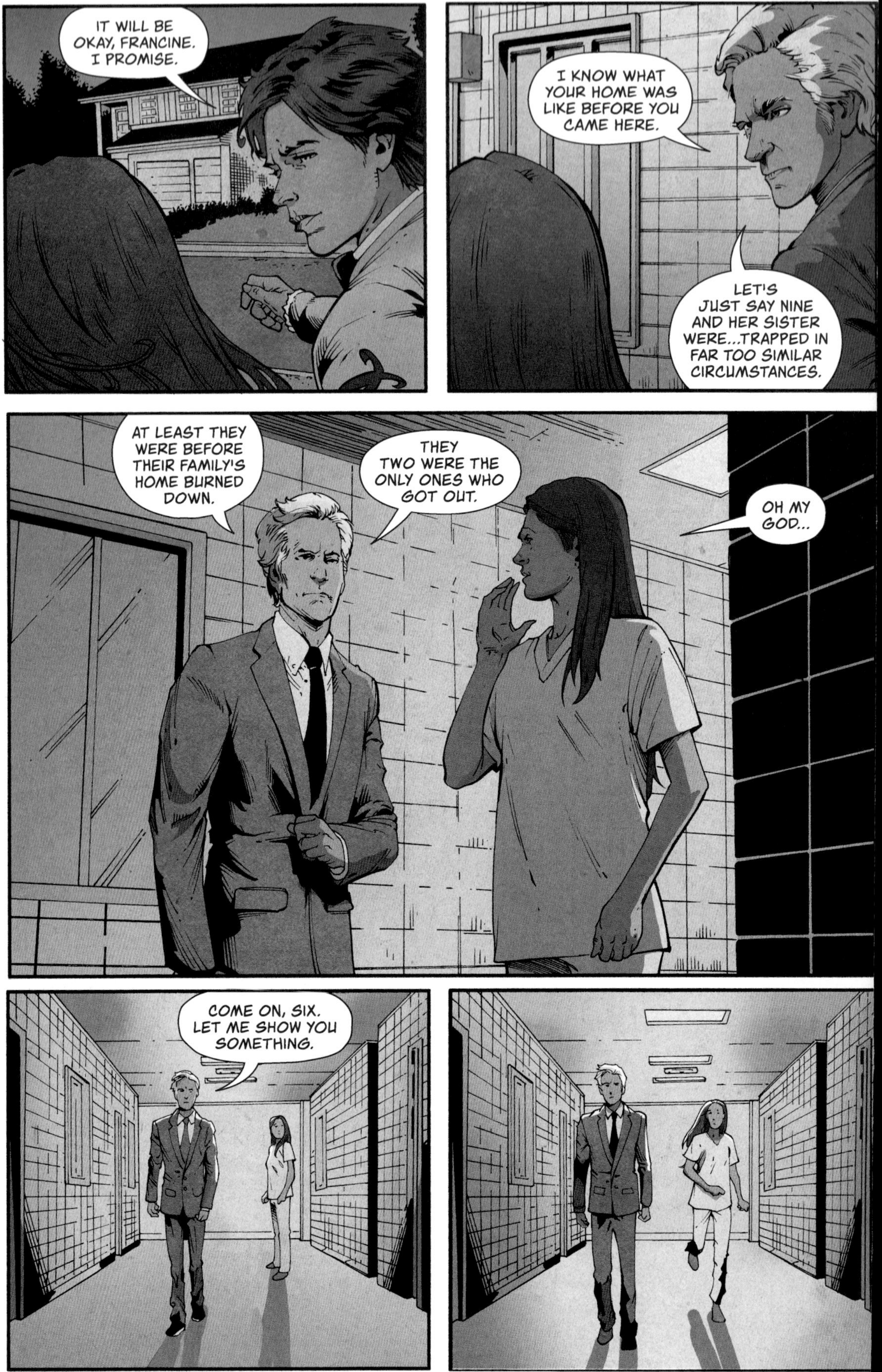
IT WILL BE OKAY, FRANCINE. I PROMISE.
I KNOW WHAT YOUR HOME WAS LIKE BEFORE YOU CAME HERE.
LET'S JUST SAY NINE AND HER SISTER WERE...TRAPPED IN FAR TOO SIMILAR CIRCUMSTANCES.
AT LEAST THEY WERE BEFORE THEIR FAMILY'S HOME BURNED DOWN.
THEY TWO WERE THE ONLY ONES WHO GOT OUT.
OH MY GOD...
COME ON, SIX. LET ME SHOW YOU SOMETHING.

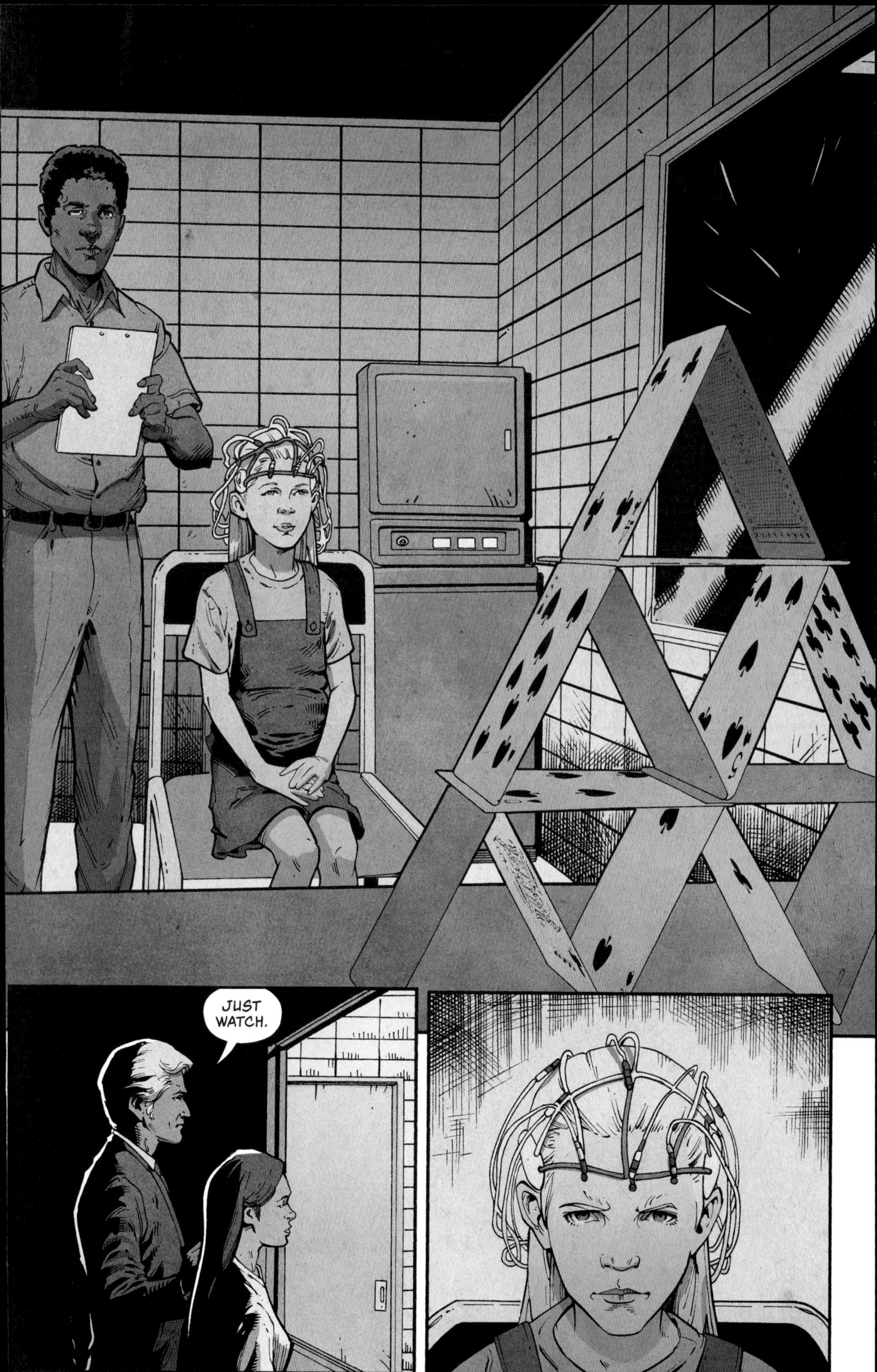
JUST WATCH.

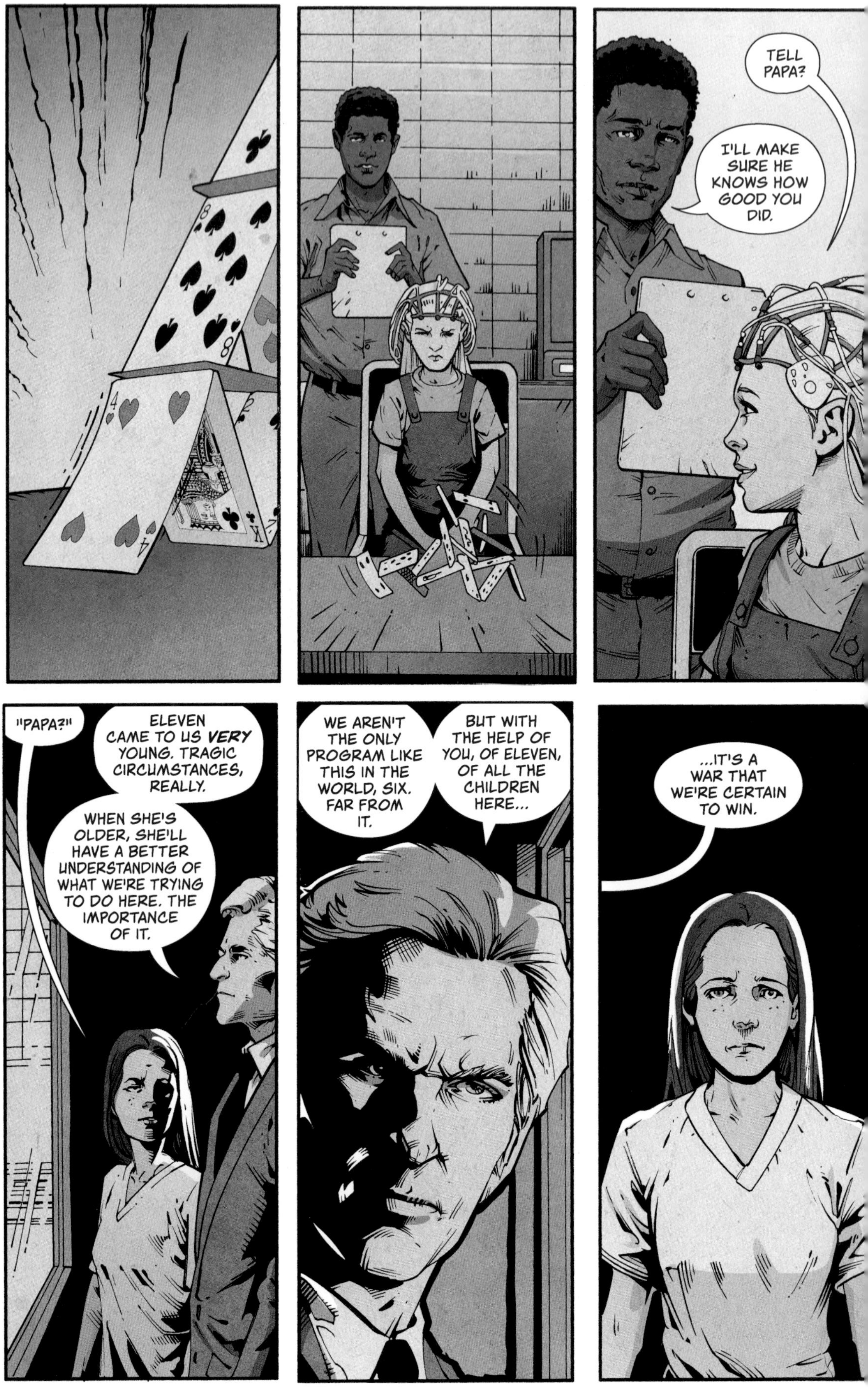

TELL PAPA?
I'LL MAKE SURE HE KNOWS HOW GOOD YOU DID.
"PAPA?"
ELEVEN CAME TO US VERY YOUNG. TRAGIC CIRCUMSTANCES, REALLY.
WHEN SHE'S OLDER, SHE'LL HAVE A BETTER UNDERSTANDING OF WHAT WE'RE TRYING TO DO HERE. THE IMPORTANCE OF IT.
WE AREN'T THE ONLY PROGRAM LIKE THIS IN THE WORLD, SIX. FAR FROM IT.
BUT WITH THE HELP OF YOU, OF ELEVEN, OF ALL THE CHILDREN HERE...
...IT'S A WAR THAT WE'RE CERTAIN TO WIN.

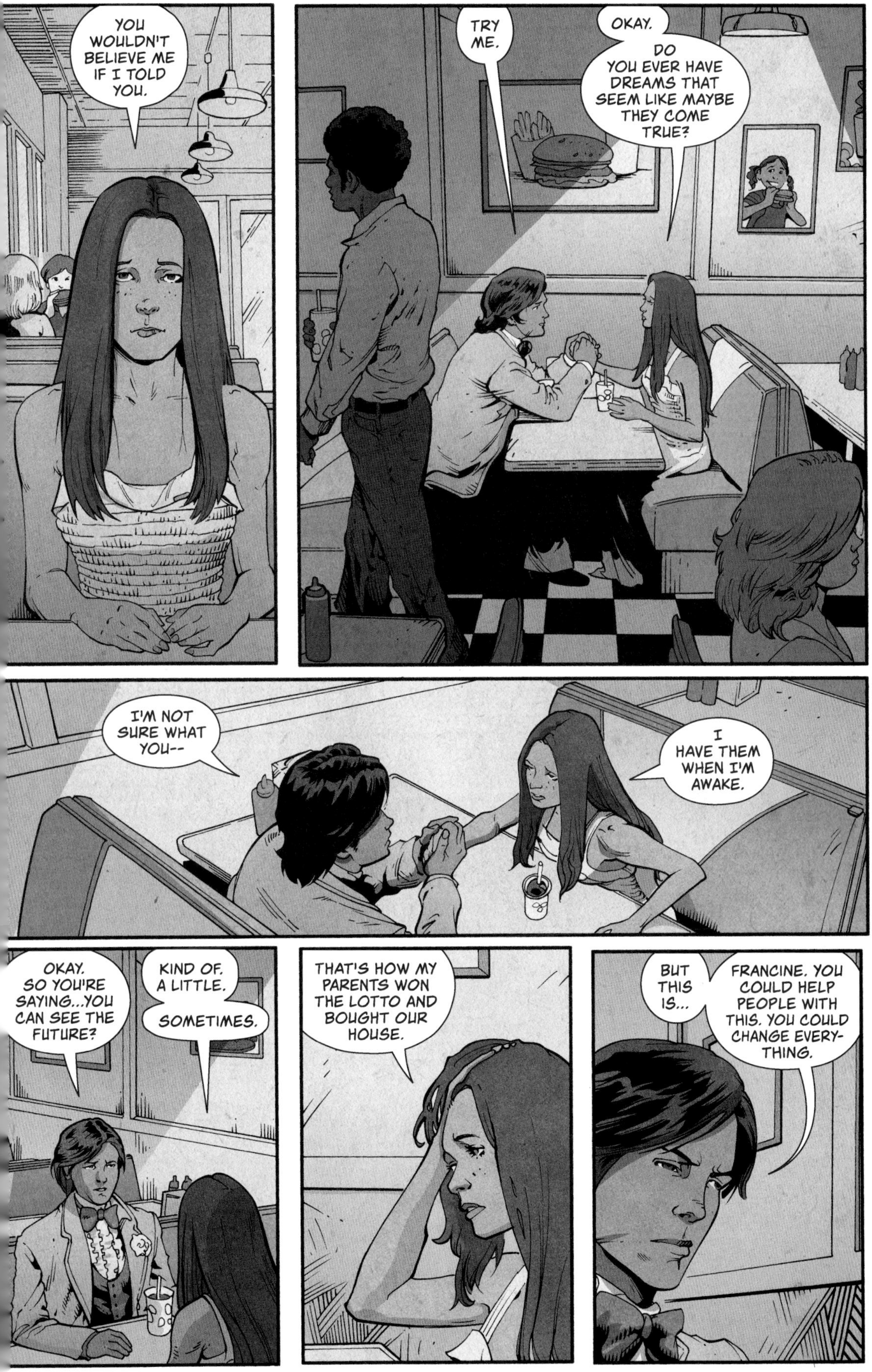

YOU WOULDN'T BELIEVE ME IF I TOLD YOU.
TRY ME.
OKAY.
DO YOU EVER HAVE DREAMS THAT SEEM LIKE MAYBE THEY COME TRUE?
I'M NOT SURE WHAT YOU--
I HAVE THEM WHEN I'M AWAKE.
OKAY. SO YOU'RE SAYING...YOU CAN SEE THE FUTURE?
KIND OF. A LITTLE.
SOMETIMES.
THAT'S HOW MY PARENTS WON THE LOTTO AND BOUGHT OUR HOUSE.
BUT THIS IS...
FRANCINE. YOU COULD HELP PEOPLE WITH THIS. YOU COULD CHANGE EVERY-THING.

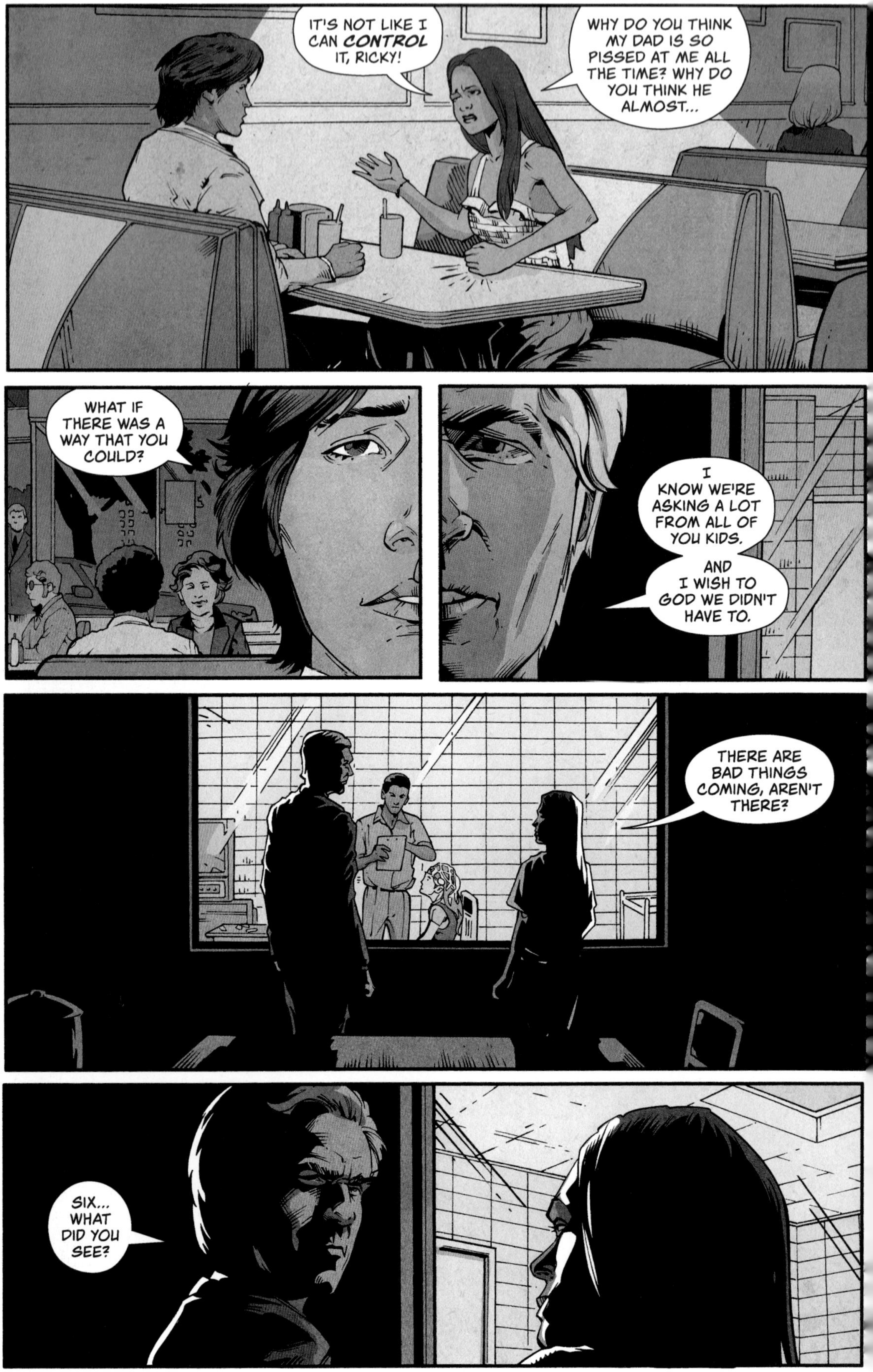
IT'S NOT LIKE I CAN CONTROL IT, RICKY!
WHY DO YOU THINK MY DAD IS SO PISSED AT ME ALL THE TIME? WHY DO YOU THINK HE ALMOST...
WHAT IF THERE WAS A WAY THAT YOU COULD?
I KNOW WE'RE ASKING A LOT FROM ALL OF YOU KIDS.
AND I WISH TO GOD WE DIDN'T HAVE TO.
THERE ARE BAD THINGS COMING, AREN'T THERE?
SIX... WHAT DID YOU SEE?

NO, I DIDN'T MEAN...

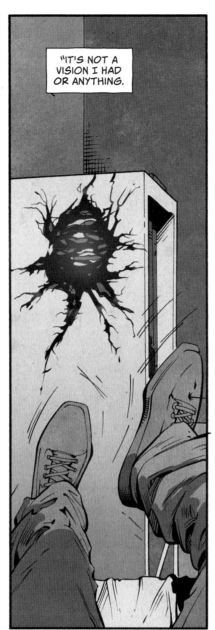

"IT'S NOT A VISION I HAD OR ANYTHING.

"MORE OF A FEELING. LIKE... SOMETHING COLD.

"SOMETHING BAD, MAYBE."

DO YOU KNOW WHAT THAT COULD BE?

NO, I CAN'T SAY THAT I DO.

BUT I HAVE A WAY WE CAN POSSIBLY FIND OUT. *IF* YOU THINK YOU'RE READY TO TAKE THE NEXT STEP.

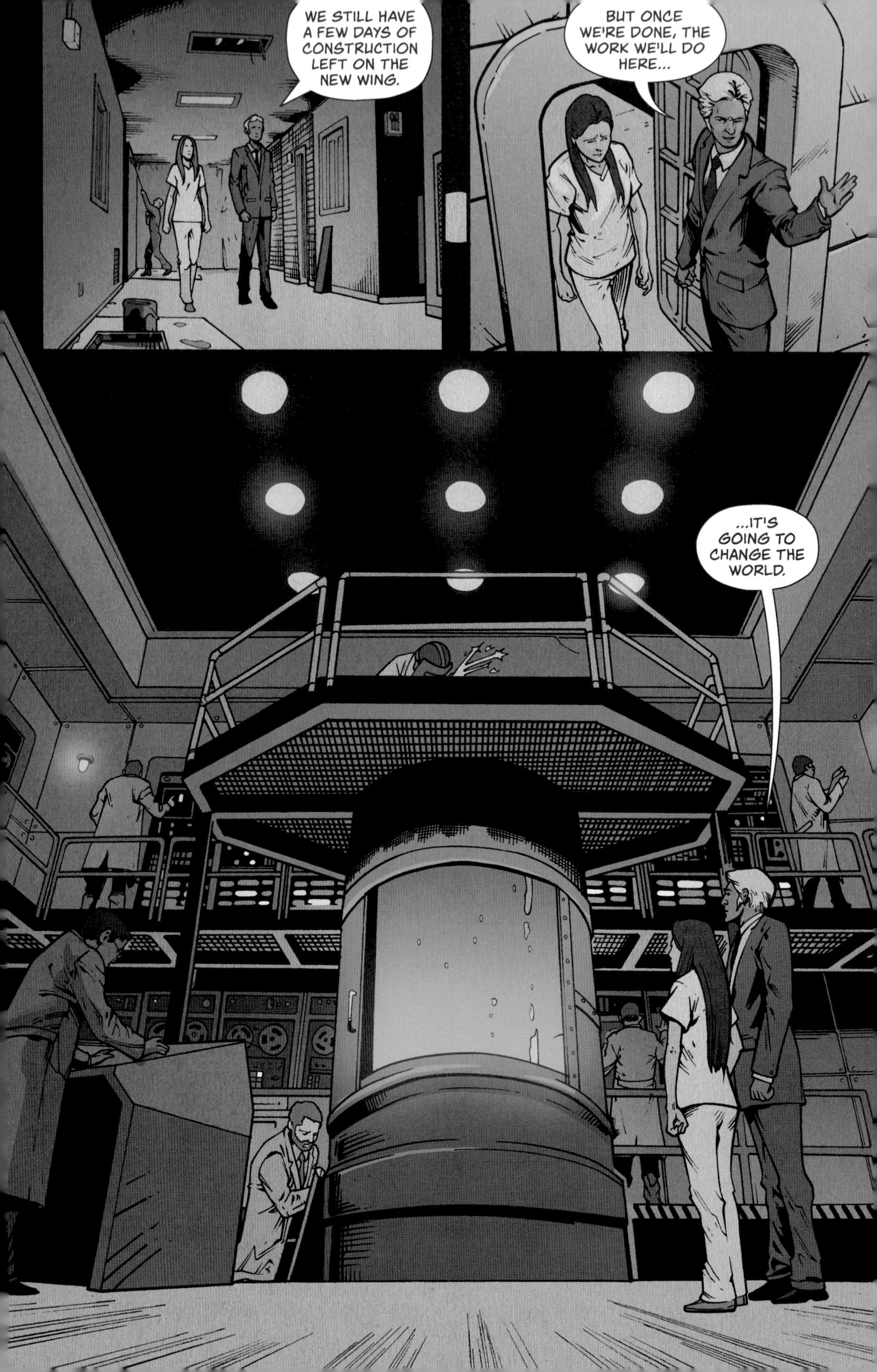
WE STILL HAVE A FEW DAYS OF CONSTRUCTION LEFT ON THE NEW WING.
BUT ONCE WE'RE DONE, THE WORK WE'LL DO HERE...
...IT'S GOING TO CHANGE THE WORLD.

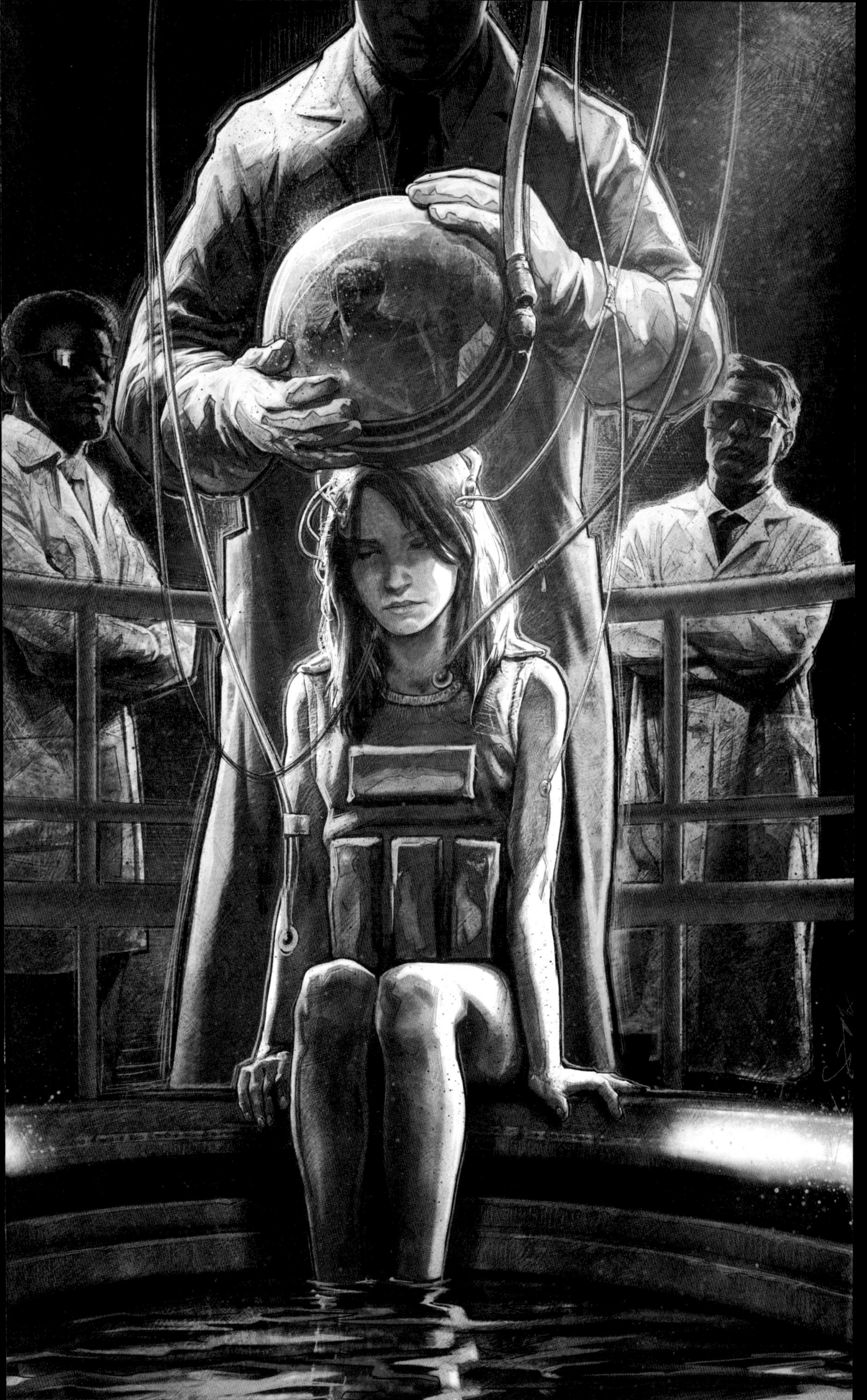

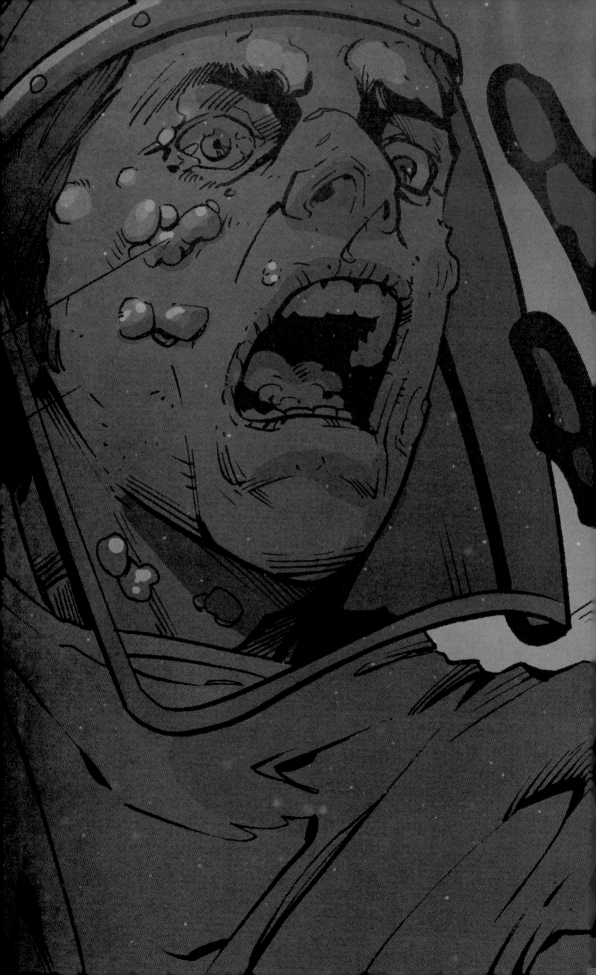

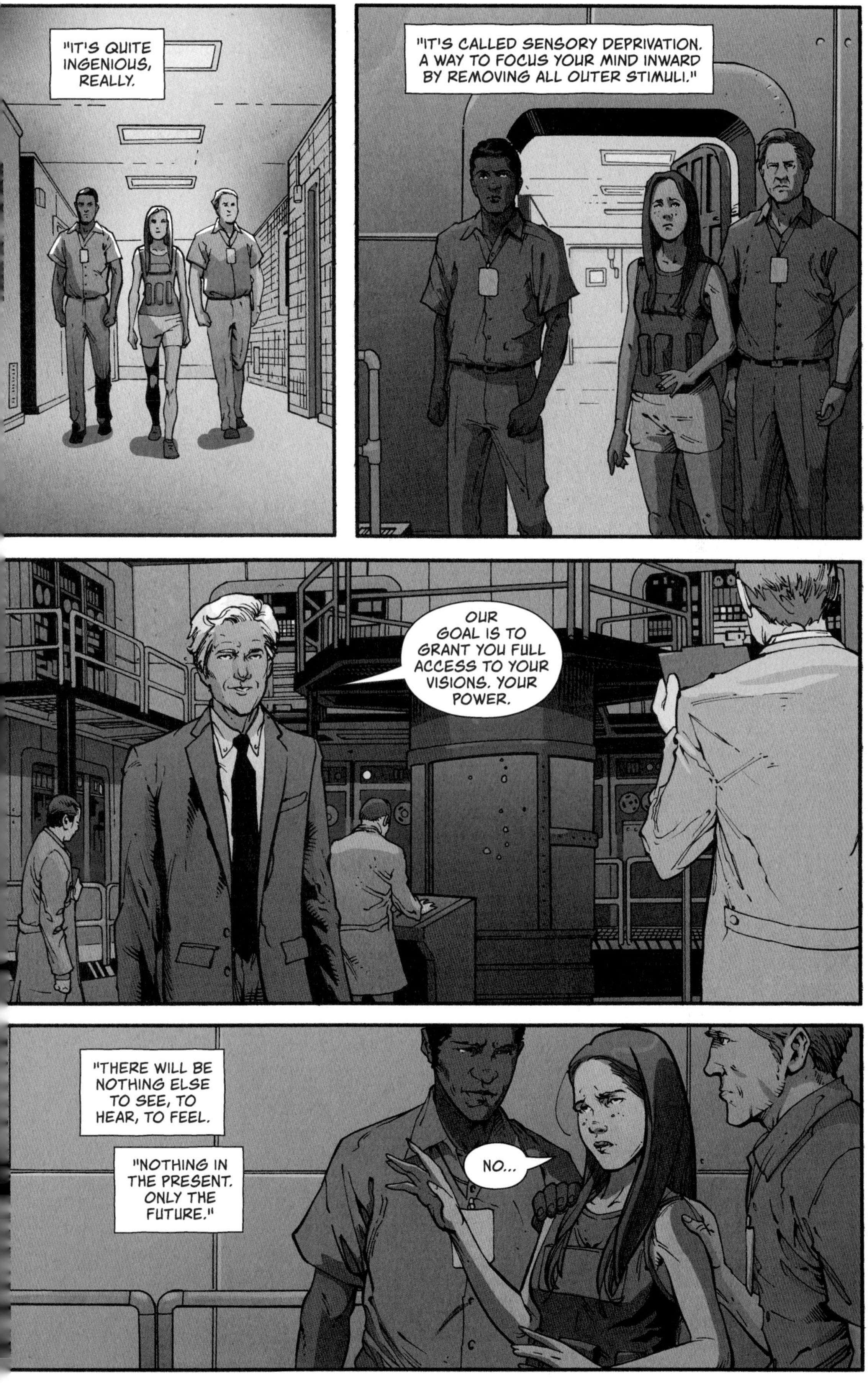
"IT'S QUITE INGENIOUS, REALLY.
"IT'S CALLED SENSORY DEPRIVATION. A WAY TO FOCUS YOUR MIND INWARD BY REMOVING ALL OUTER STIMULI."
OUR GOAL IS TO GRANT YOU FULL ACCESS TO YOUR VISIONS. YOUR POWER.
"THERE WILL BE NOTHING ELSE TO SEE, TO HEAR, TO FEEL.
"NOTHING IN THE PRESENT. ONLY THE FUTURE."
NO...

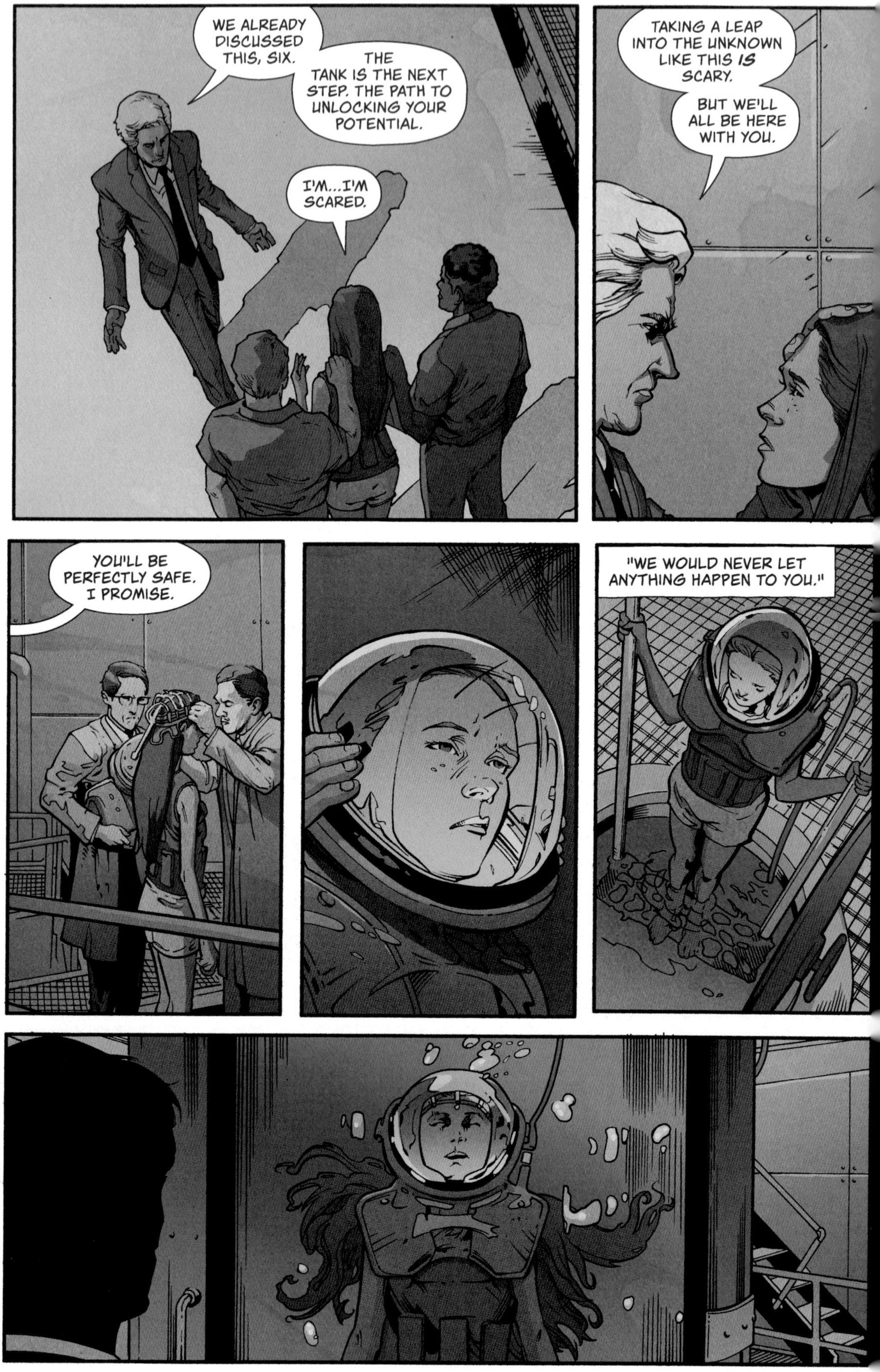
WE ALREADY DISCUSSED THIS, SIX.
THE TANK IS THE NEXT STEP. THE PATH TO UNLOCKING YOUR POTENTIAL.
I'M...I'M SCARED.
TAKING A LEAP INTO THE UNKNOWN LIKE THIS IS SCARY.
BUT WE'LL ALL BE HERE WITH YOU.
YOU'LL BE PERFECTLY SAFE. I PROMISE.
"WE WOULD NEVER LET ANYTHING HAPPEN TO YOU."

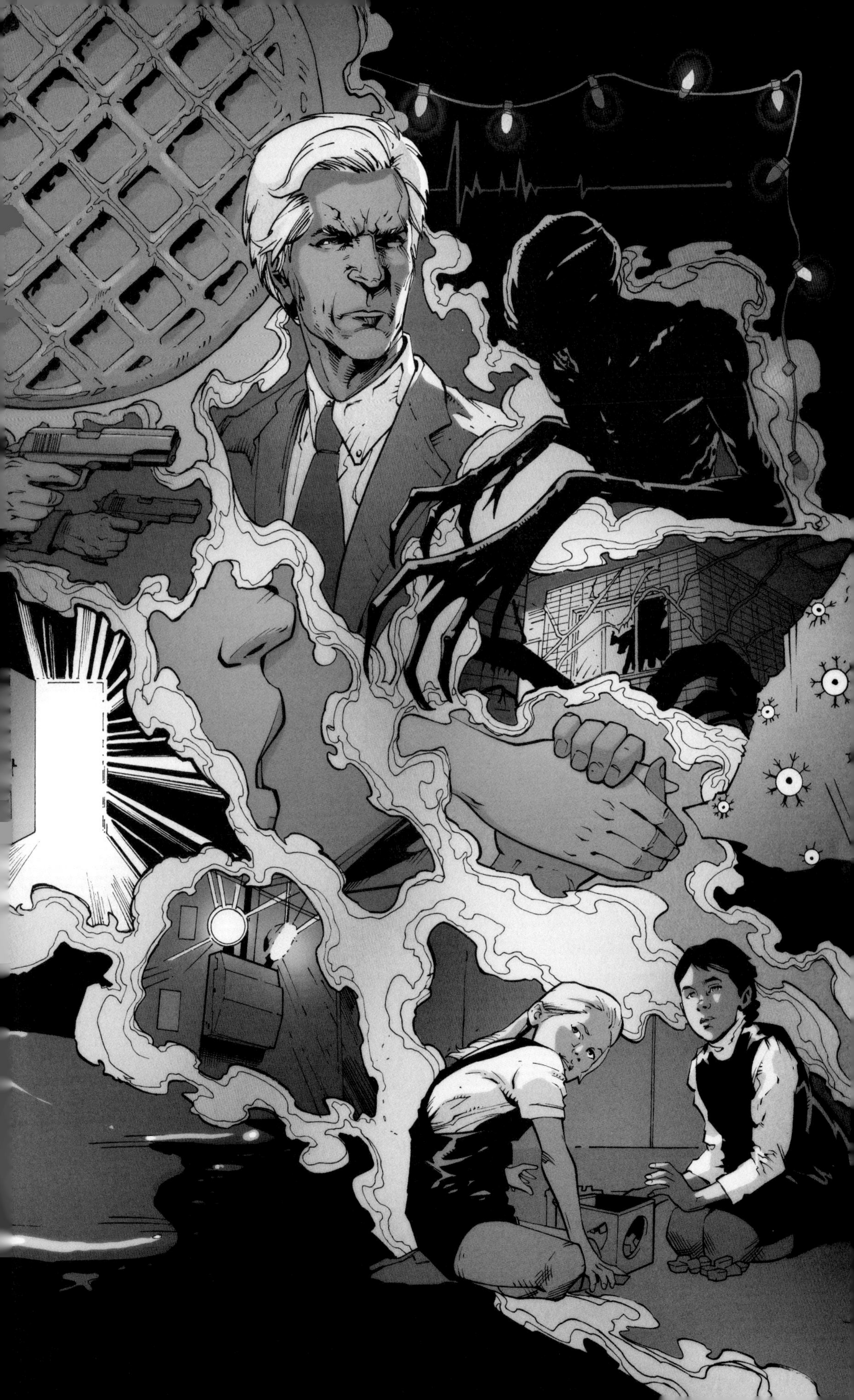

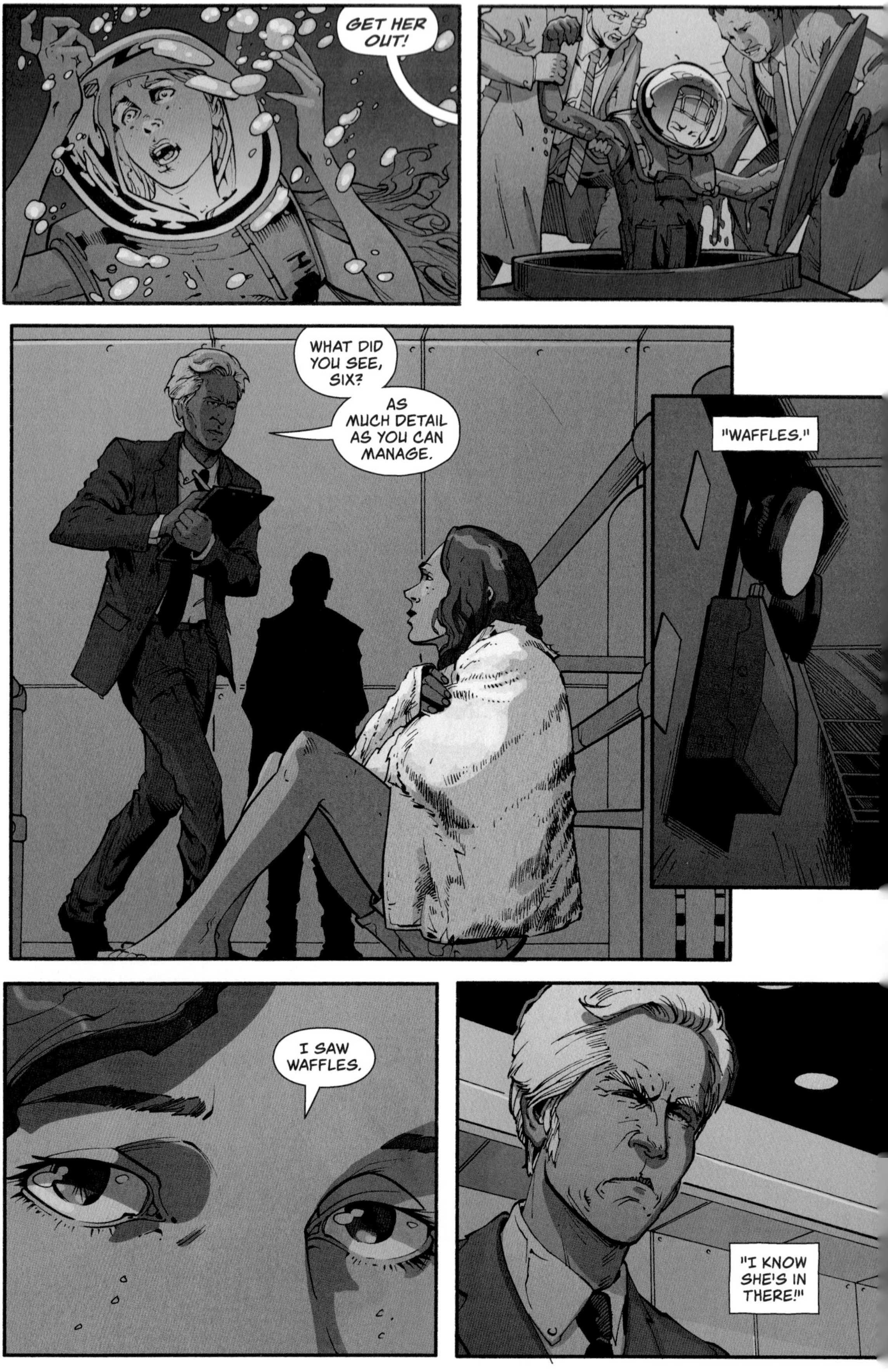
GET HER OUT!
WHAT DID YOU SEE, SIX?
AS MUCH DETAIL AS YOU CAN MANAGE.
"WAFFLES."
I SAW WAFFLES.
"I KNOW SHE'S IN THERE!"

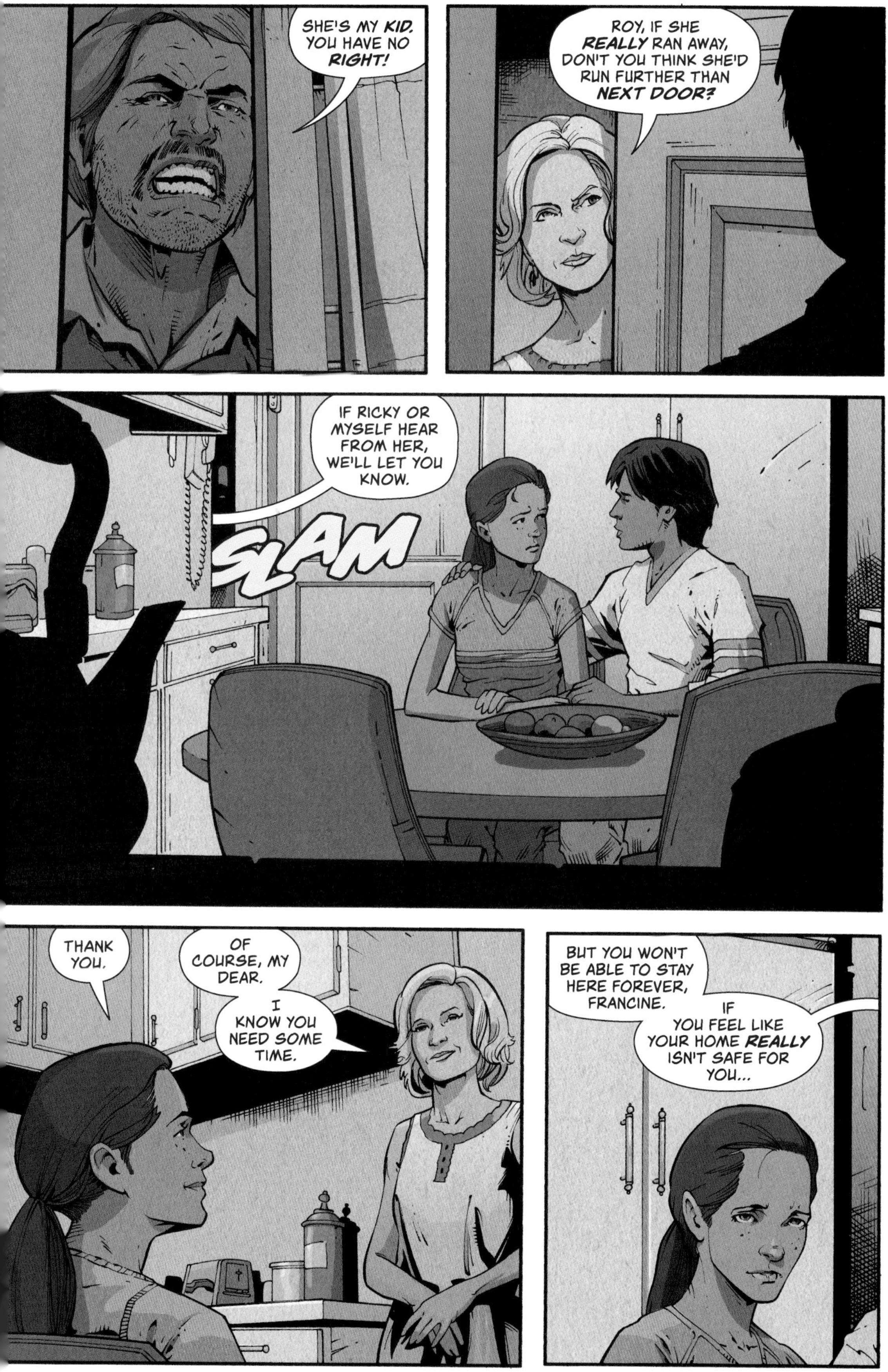
SHE'S MY KID. YOU HAVE NO RIGHT!
ROY, IF SHE REALLY RAN AWAY, DON'T YOU THINK SHE'D RUN FURTHER THAN NEXT DOOR?
IF RICKY OR MYSELF HEAR FROM HER, WE'LL LET YOU KNOW.
SLAM
THANK YOU.
OF COURSE, MY DEAR.
I KNOW YOU NEED SOME TIME.
BUT YOU WON'T BE ABLE TO STAY HERE FOREVER, FRANCINE.
IF YOU FEEL LIKE YOUR HOME REALLY ISN'T SAFE FOR YOU...

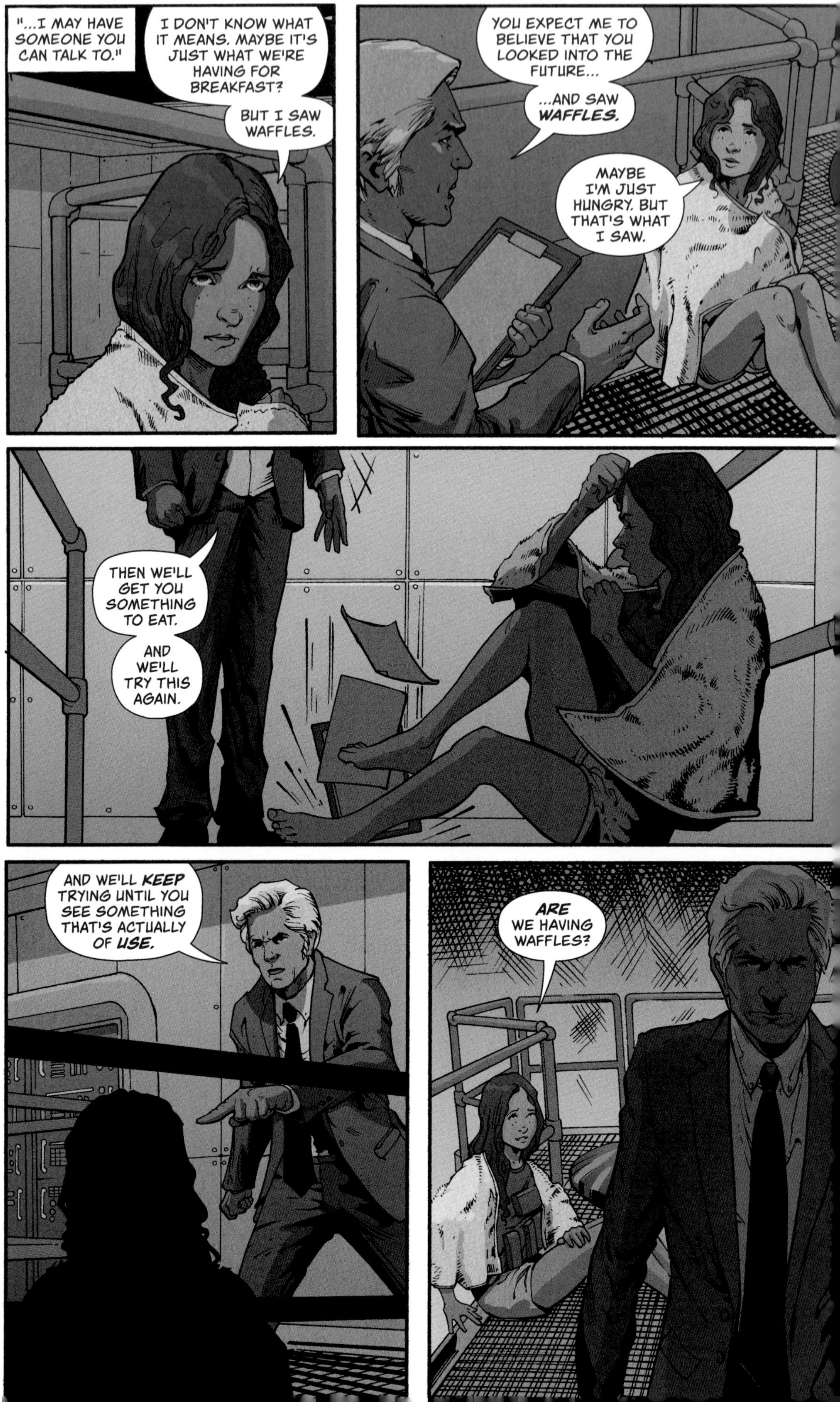
"...I MAY HAVE SOMEONE YOU CAN TALK TO."
I DON'T KNOW WHAT IT MEANS. MAYBE IT'S JUST WHAT WE'RE HAVING FOR BREAKFAST?
BUT I SAW WAFFLES.
YOU EXPECT ME TO BELIEVE THAT YOU LOOKED INTO THE FUTURE...
...AND SAW *WAFFLES.*
MAYBE I'M JUST HUNGRY. BUT THAT'S WHAT I SAW.
THEN WE'LL GET YOU SOMETHING TO EAT.
AND WE'LL TRY THIS AGAIN.
AND WE'LL *KEEP* TRYING UNTIL YOU SEE SOMETHING THAT'S ACTUALLY OF *USE.*
ARE WE HAVING WAFFLES?

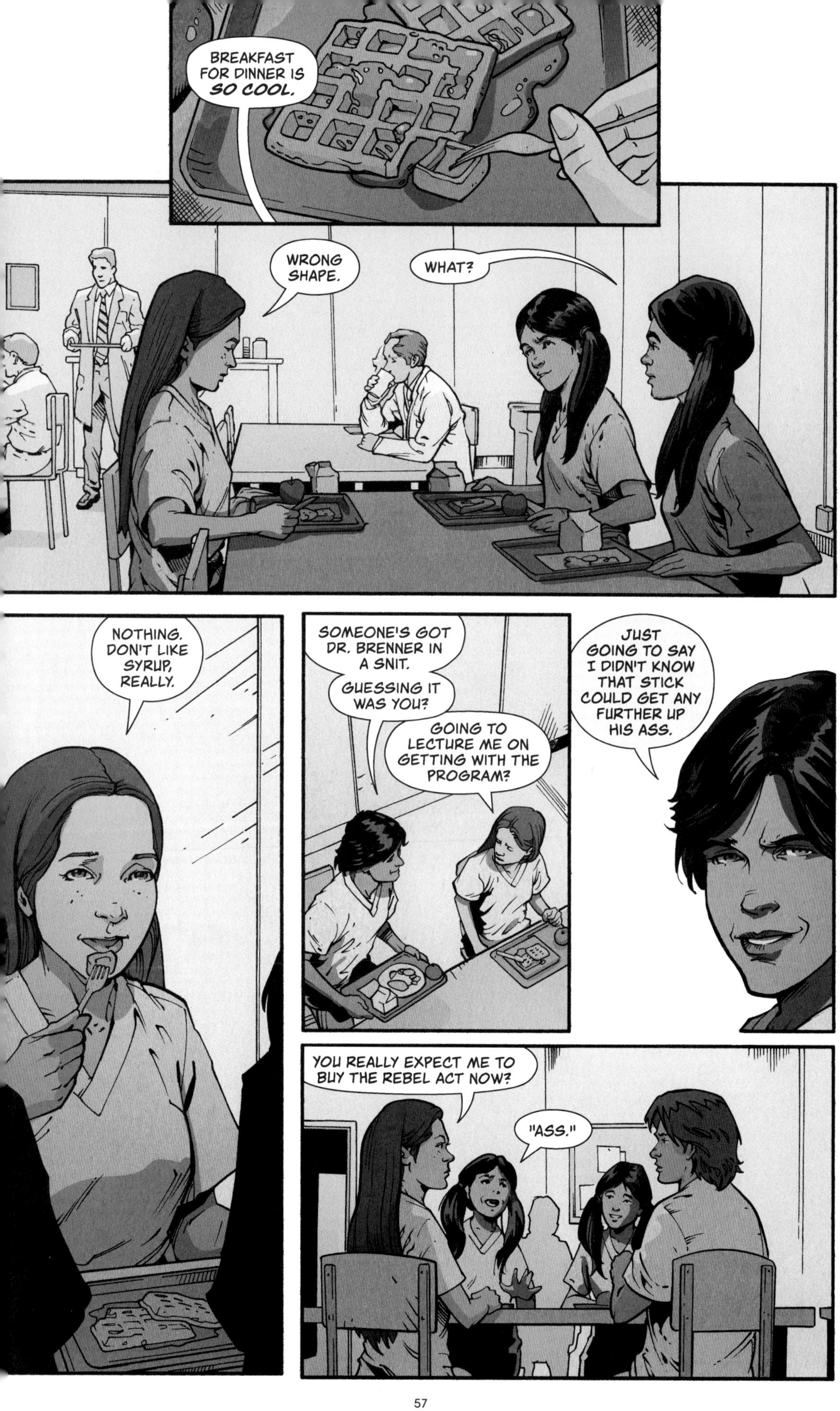
BREAKFAST FOR DINNER IS SO COOL.
WRONG SHAPE.
WHAT?
NOTHING. DON'T LIKE SYRUP, REALLY.
SOMEONE'S GOT DR. BRENNER IN A SNIT.
GUESSING IT WAS YOU?
GOING TO LECTURE ME ON GETTING WITH THE PROGRAM?
JUST GOING TO SAY I DIDN'T KNOW THAT STICK COULD GET ANY FURTHER UP HIS ASS.
YOU REALLY EXPECT ME TO BUY THE REBEL ACT NOW?
"ASS."

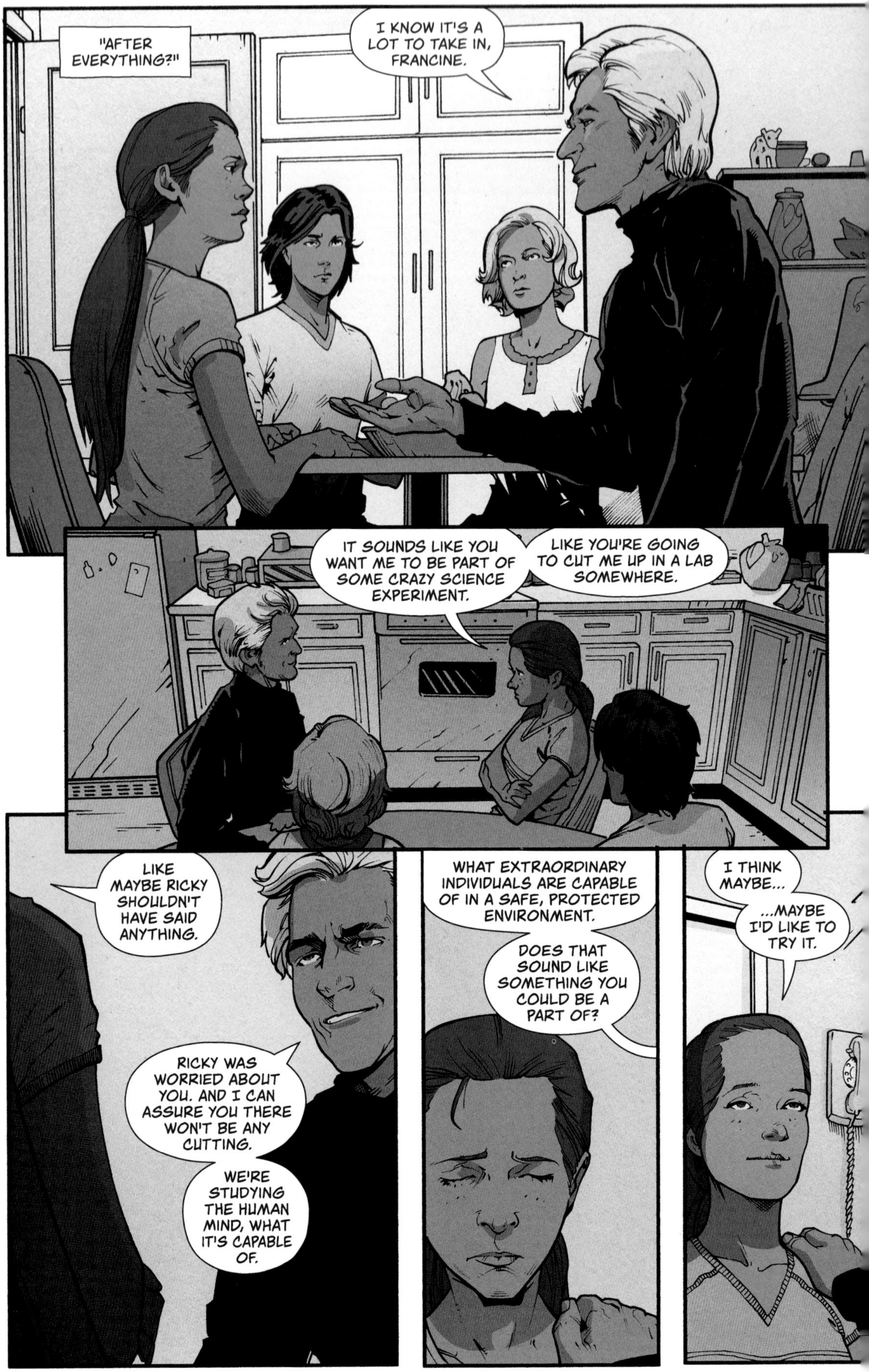
"AFTER EVERYTHING?"
I KNOW IT'S A LOT TO TAKE IN, FRANCINE.
IT SOUNDS LIKE YOU WANT ME TO BE PART OF SOME CRAZY SCIENCE EXPERIMENT.
LIKE YOU'RE GOING TO CUT ME UP IN A LAB SOMEWHERE.
LIKE MAYBE RICKY SHOULDN'T HAVE SAID ANYTHING.
RICKY WAS WORRIED ABOUT YOU. AND I CAN ASSURE YOU THERE WON'T BE ANY CUTTING.
WE'RE STUDYING THE HUMAN MIND, WHAT IT'S CAPABLE OF.
WHAT EXTRAORDINARY INDIVIDUALS ARE CAPABLE OF IN A SAFE, PROTECTED ENVIRONMENT.
DOES THAT SOUND LIKE SOMETHING YOU COULD BE A PART OF?
I THINK MAYBE...
...MAYBE I'D LIKE TO TRY IT.

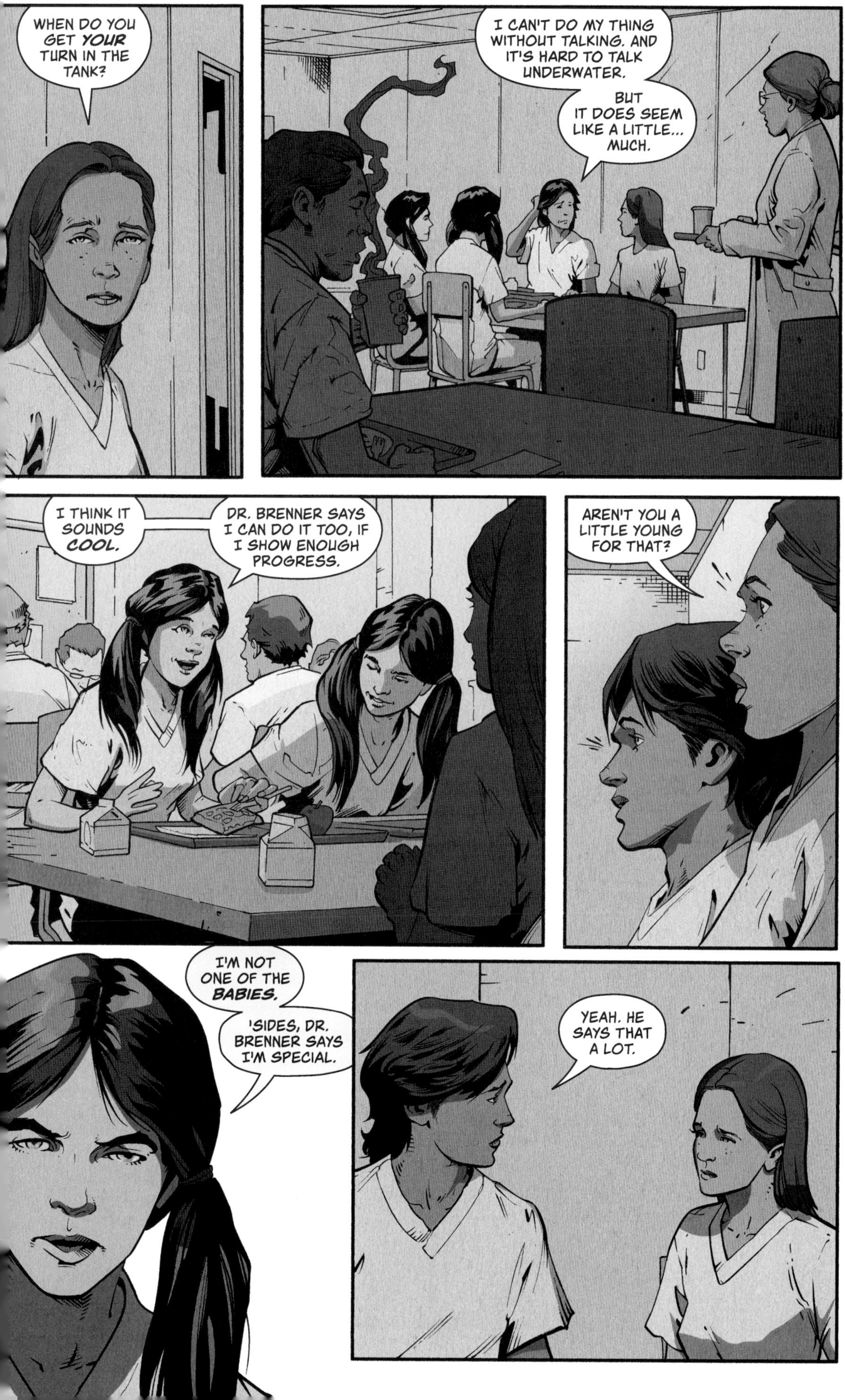
WHEN DO YOU GET YOUR TURN IN THE TANK?
I CAN'T DO MY THING WITHOUT TALKING. AND IT'S HARD TO TALK UNDERWATER.
BUT IT DOES SEEM LIKE A LITTLE... MUCH.
I THINK IT SOUNDS COOL.
DR. BRENNER SAYS I CAN DO IT TOO, IF I SHOW ENOUGH PROGRESS.
AREN'T YOU A LITTLE YOUNG FOR THAT?
I'M NOT ONE OF THE BABIES.
'SIDES, DR. BRENNER SAYS I'M SPECIAL.
YEAH. HE SAYS THAT A LOT.

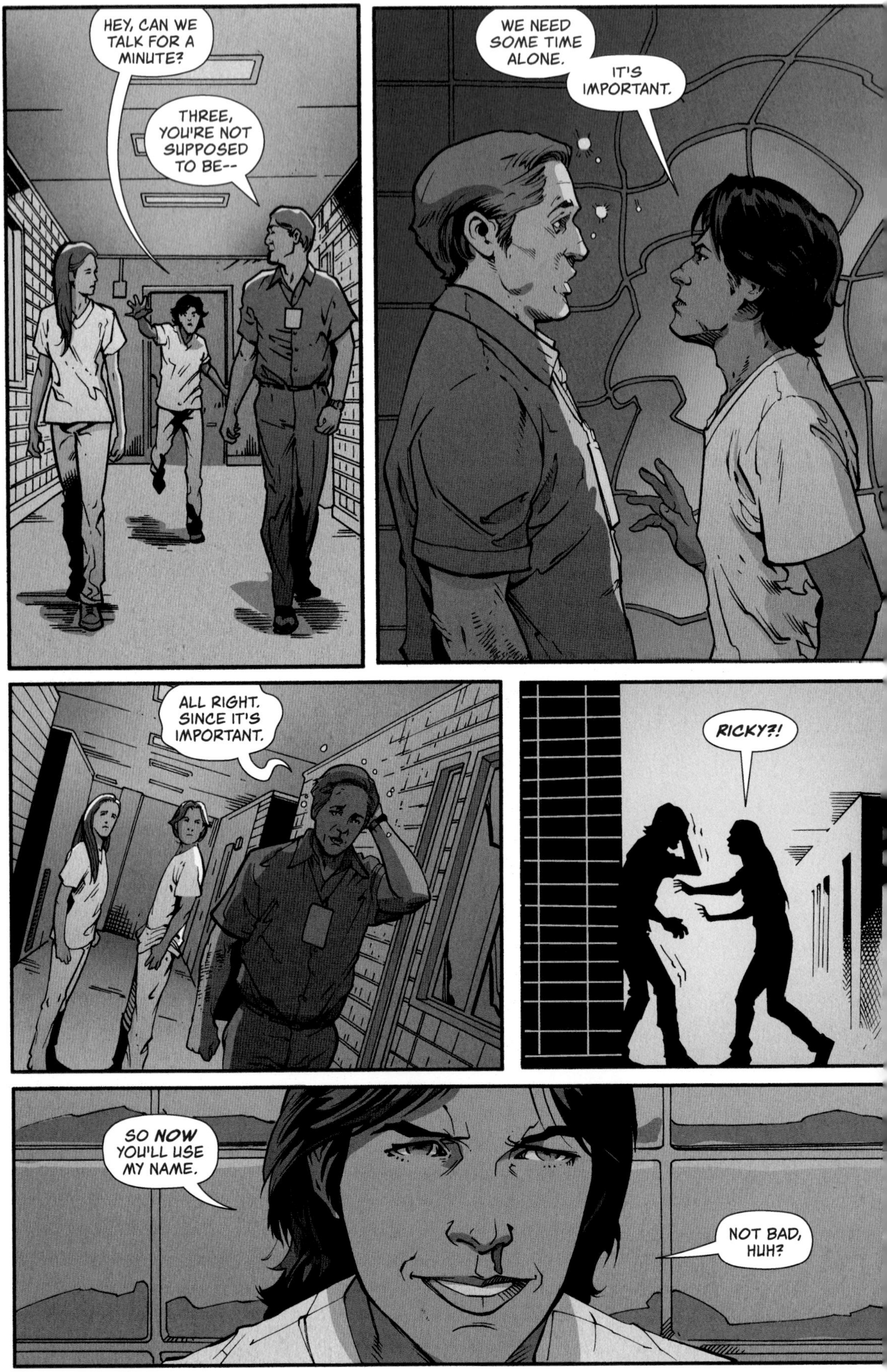
HEY, CAN WE TALK FOR A MINUTE?
THREE, YOU'RE NOT SUPPOSED TO BE--
WE NEED SOME TIME ALONE.
IT'S IMPORTANT.
ALL RIGHT. SINCE IT'S IMPORTANT.
RICKY?!
SO NOW YOU'LL USE MY NAME.
NOT BAD, HUH?

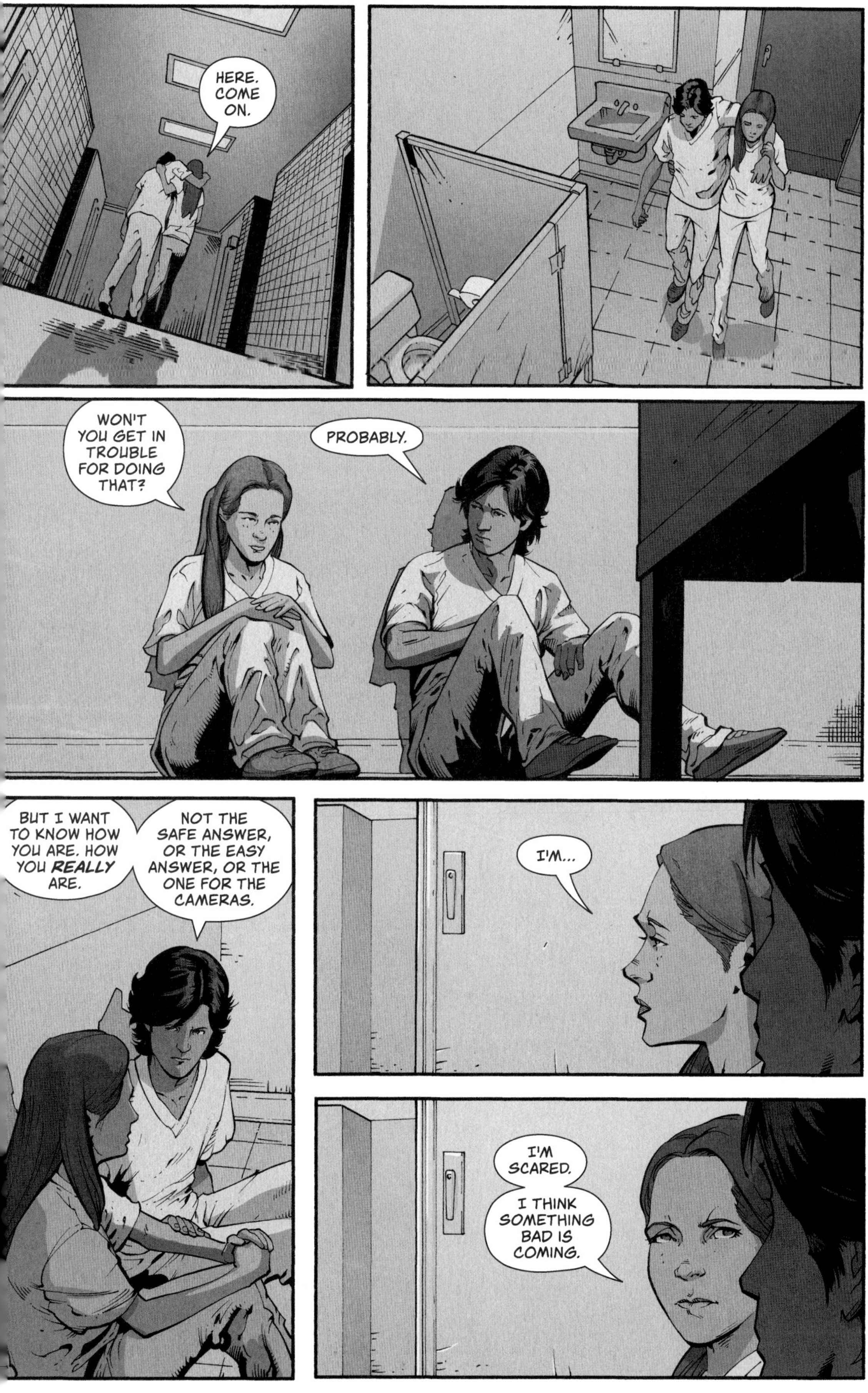
HERE. COME ON.
WON'T YOU GET IN TROUBLE FOR DOING THAT?
PROBABLY.
BUT I WANT TO KNOW HOW YOU ARE. HOW YOU **REALLY** ARE.
NOT THE SAFE ANSWER, OR THE EASY ANSWER, OR THE ONE FOR THE CAMERAS.
I'M...
I'M SCARED.
I THINK SOMETHING BAD IS COMING.

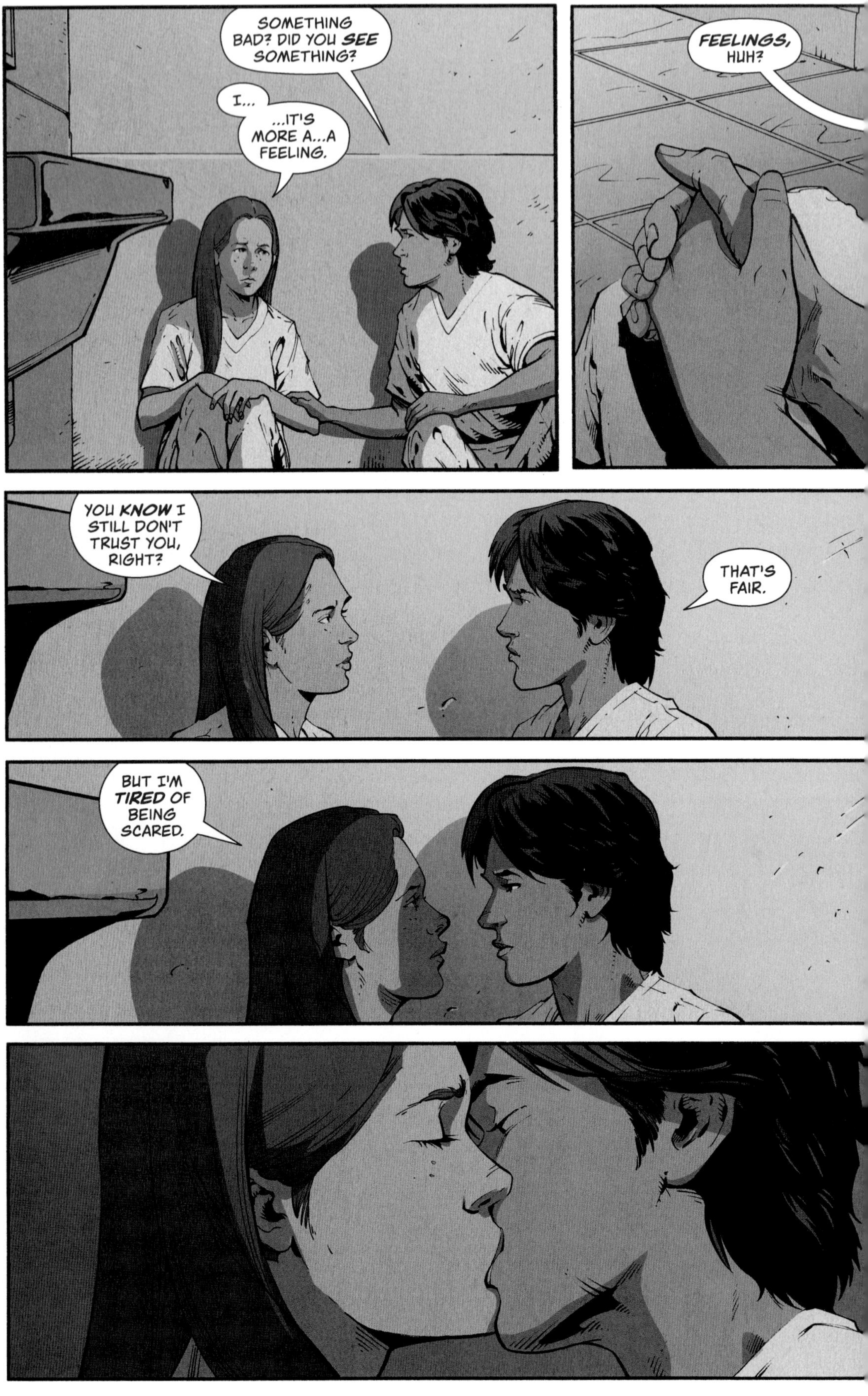
SOMETHING BAD? DID YOU SEE SOMETHING?
I...
...IT'S MORE A...A FEELING.
FEELINGS, HUH?
YOU KNOW I STILL DON'T TRUST YOU, RIGHT?
THAT'S FAIR.
BUT I'M TIRED OF BEING SCARED.

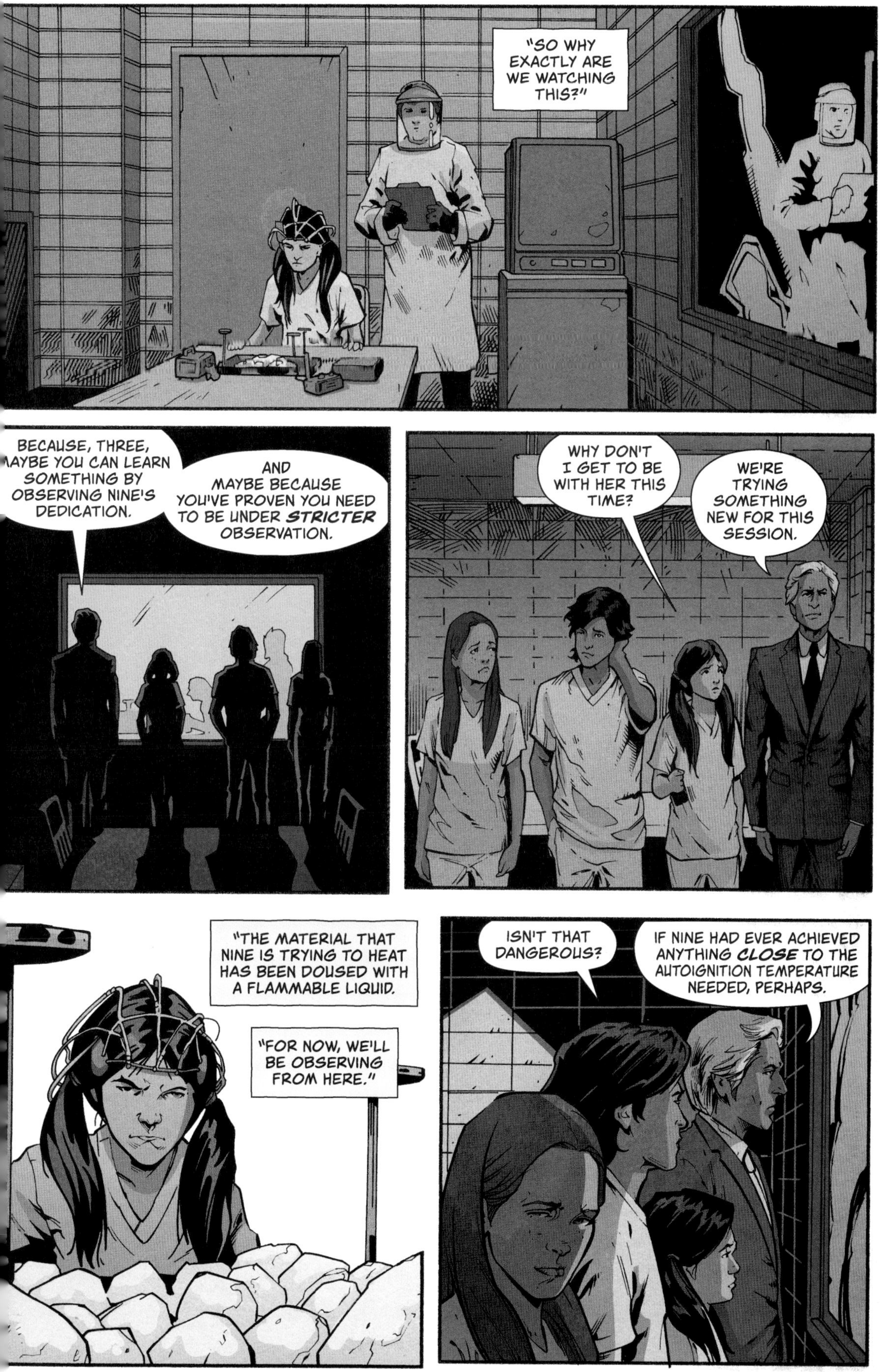
"SO WHY EXACTLY ARE WE WATCHING THIS?"
BECAUSE, THREE, AYBE YOU CAN LEARN SOMETHING BY OBSERVING NINE'S DEDICATION.
AND MAYBE BECAUSE YOU'VE PROVEN YOU NEED TO BE UNDER STRICTER OBSERVATION.
WHY DON'T I GET TO BE WITH HER THIS TIME?
WE'RE TRYING SOMETHING NEW FOR THIS SESSION.
"THE MATERIAL THAT NINE IS TRYING TO HEAT HAS BEEN DOUSED WITH A FLAMMABLE LIQUID.
"FOR NOW, WE'LL BE OBSERVING FROM HERE."
ISN'T THAT DANGEROUS?
IF NINE HAD EVER ACHIEVED ANYTHING CLOSE TO THE AUTOIGNITION TEMPERATURE NEEDED, PERHAPS.

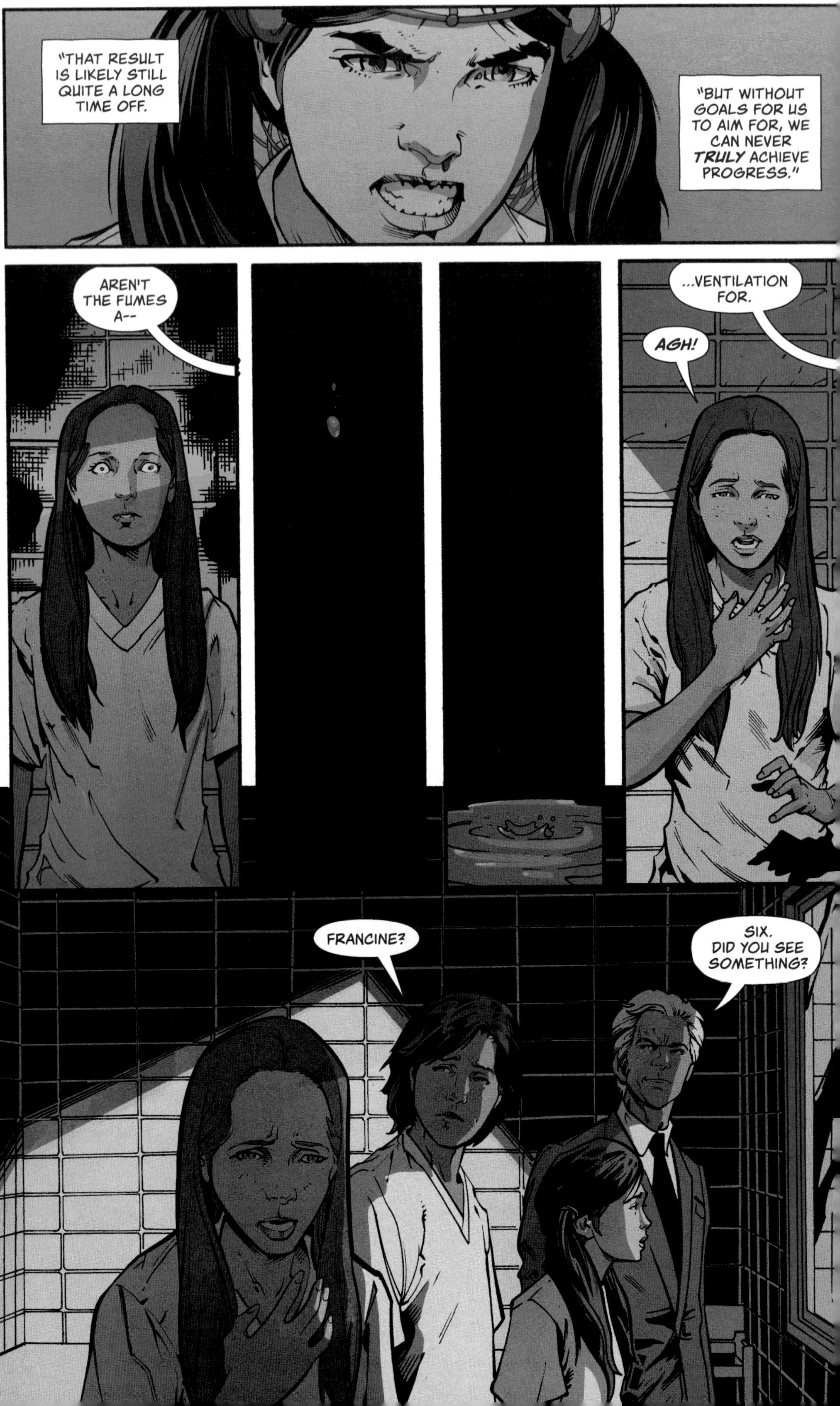
"THAT RESULT IS LIKELY STILL QUITE A LONG TIME OFF.
"BUT WITHOUT GOALS FOR US TO AIM FOR, WE CAN NEVER TRULY ACHIEVE PROGRESS."
AREN'T THE FUMES A--
...VENTILATION FOR.
AGH!
FRANCINE?
SIX. DID YOU SEE SOMETHING?

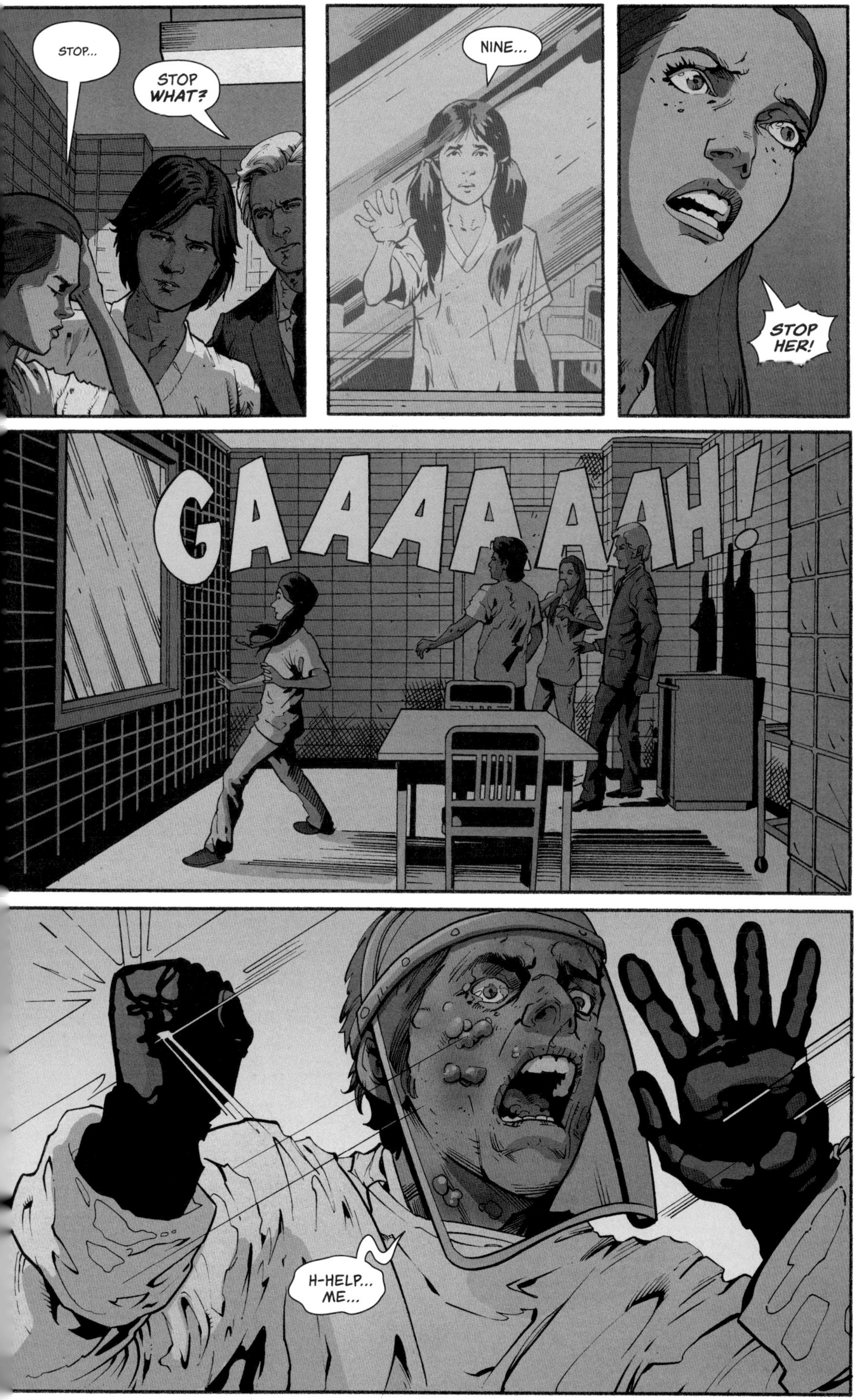
STOP...
STOP WHAT?
NINE...
STOP HER!
GAAAAAH!
H-HELP... ME...

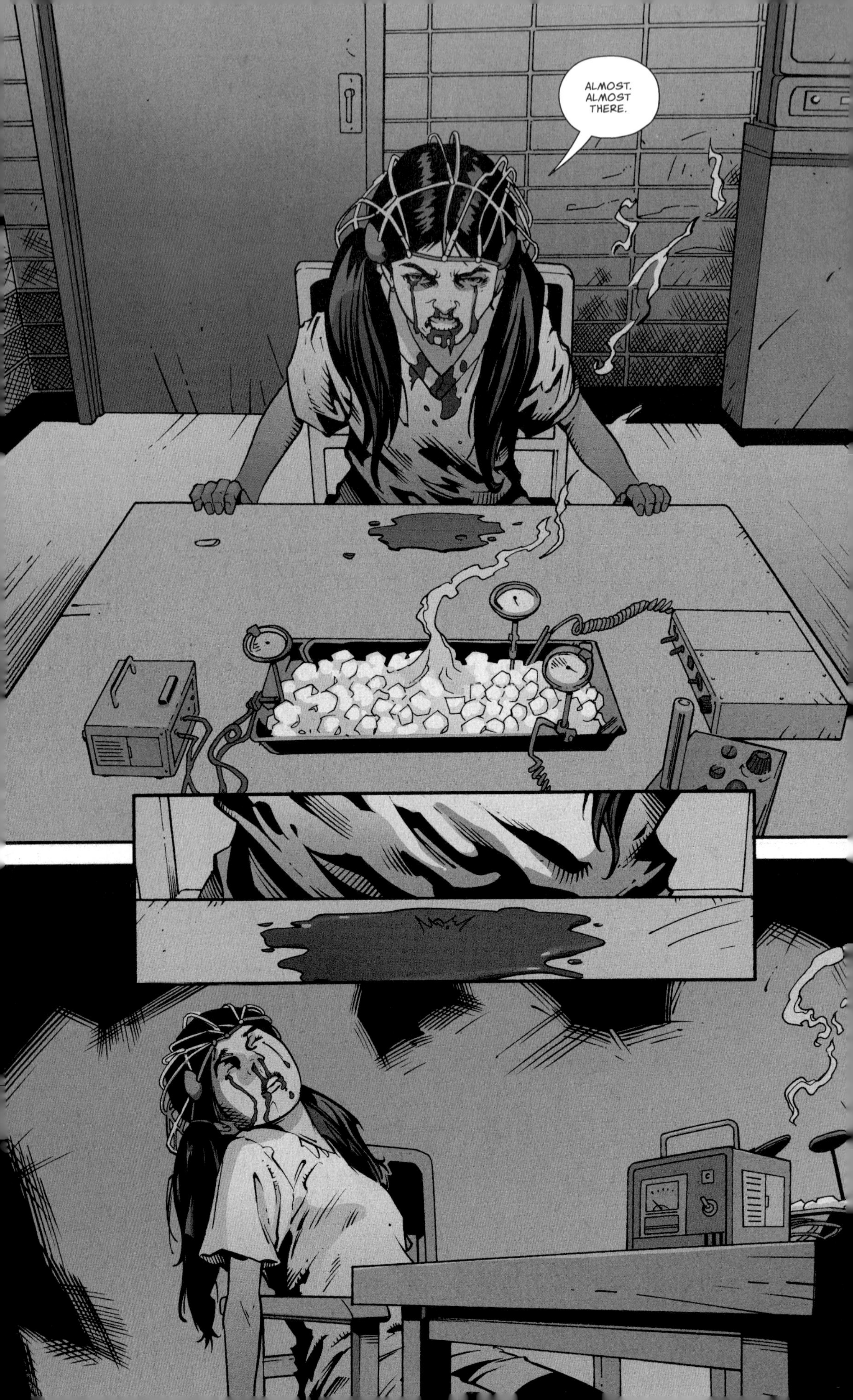
ALMOST. ALMOST THERE.

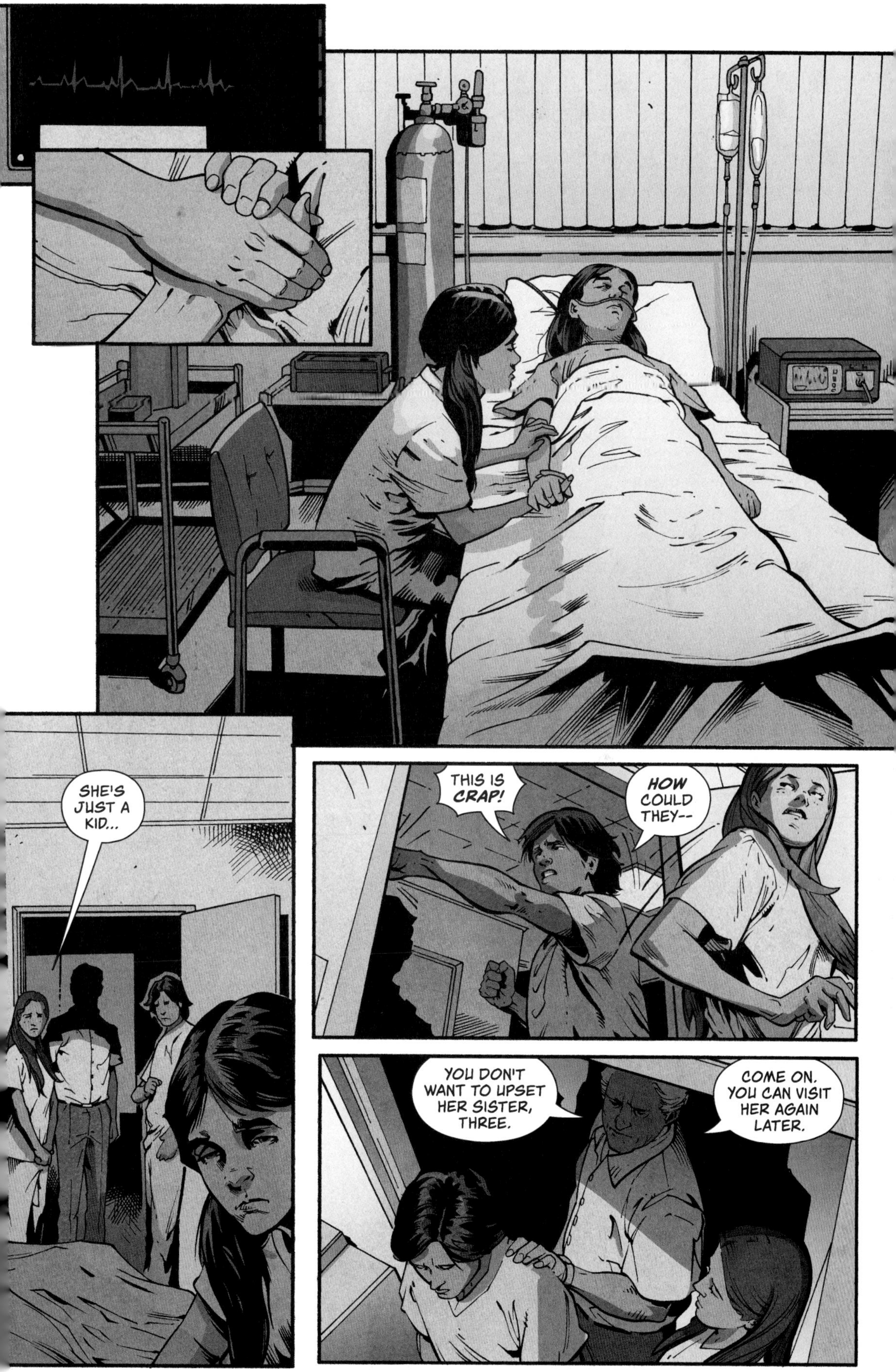
SHE'S JUST A KID...
THIS IS CRAP!
HOW COULD THEY--
YOU DON'T WANT TO UPSET HER SISTER, THREE.
COME ON. YOU CAN VISIT HER AGAIN LATER.

rap rap

CAN WE TALK, SIX?

DO I HAVE A *CHOICE?*

I KNOW WE'RE ALL UPSET ABOUT WHAT HAPPENED.

HOW DID IT HAPPEN?

WE'RE STILL TRYING TO FIGURE THAT OUT.

OUR BEST GUESS IS THAT SHE PUSHED TOO HARD AND HER POWER ESCAPED HER CONTROL.

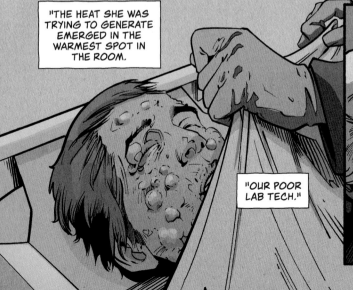

"THE HEAT SHE WAS TRYING TO GENERATE EMERGED IN THE WARMEST SPOT IN THE ROOM.

"OUR POOR LAB TECH."

WE'RE HOPING SHE'LL WAKE UP SOON AND BE ABLE TO TELL US HERSELF.

AND IF SHE DOESN'T?

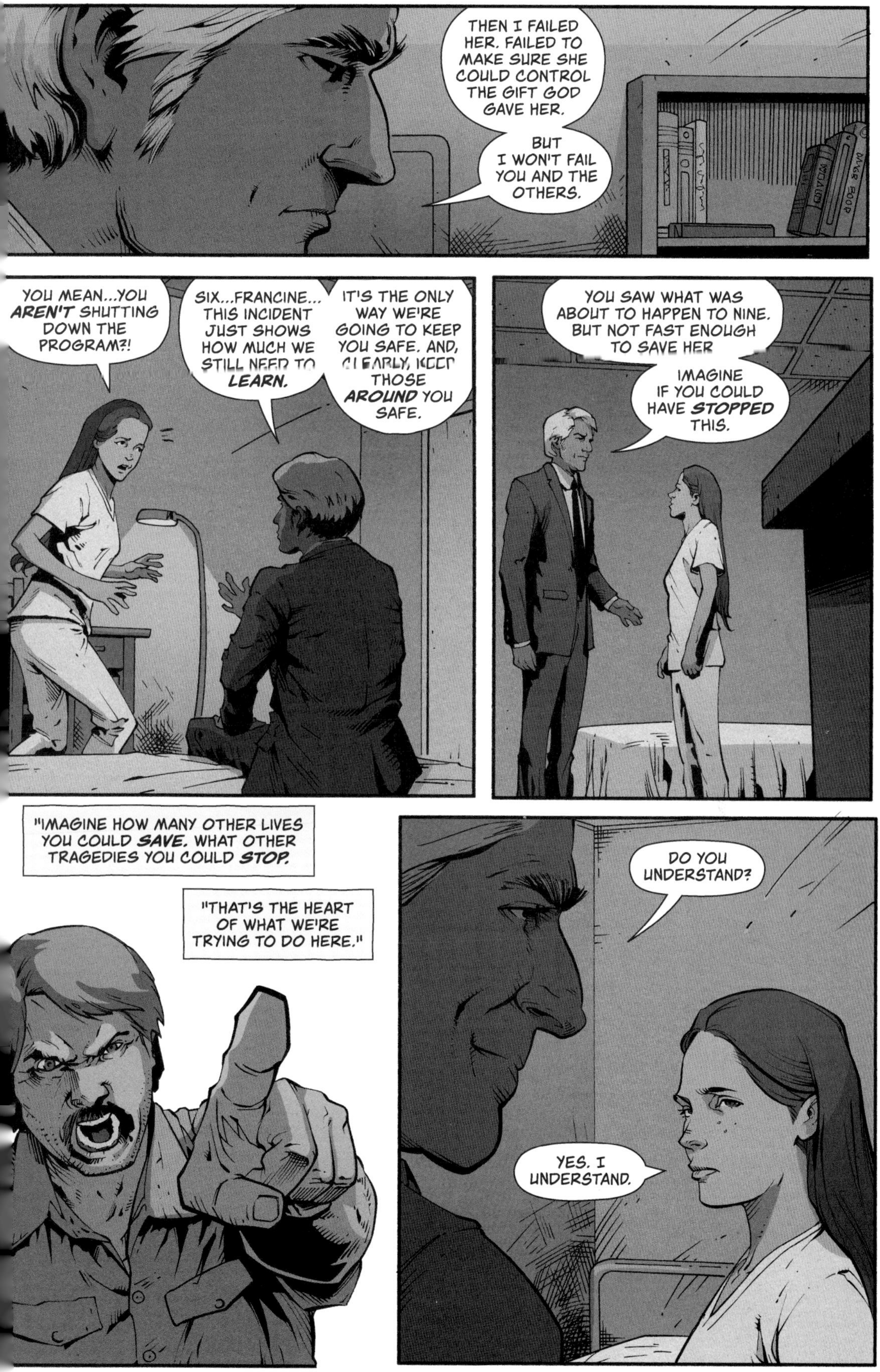
THEN I FAILED HER. FAILED TO MAKE SURE SHE COULD CONTROL THE GIFT GOD GAVE HER.
BUT I WON'T FAIL YOU AND THE OTHERS.
YOU MEAN...YOU AREN'T SHUTTING DOWN THE PROGRAM?!
SIX...FRANCINE... THIS INCIDENT JUST SHOWS HOW MUCH WE STILL NEED TO LEARN.
IT'S THE ONLY WAY WE'RE GOING TO KEEP YOU SAFE. AND, CLEARLY, KEEP THOSE AROUND YOU SAFE.
YOU SAW WHAT WAS ABOUT TO HAPPEN TO NINE. BUT NOT FAST ENOUGH TO SAVE HER.
IMAGINE IF YOU COULD HAVE STOPPED THIS.
"IMAGINE HOW MANY OTHER LIVES YOU COULD SAVE. WHAT OTHER TRAGEDIES YOU COULD STOP.
"THAT'S THE HEART OF WHAT WE'RE TRYING TO DO HERE."
DO YOU UNDERSTAND?
YES. I UNDERSTAND.

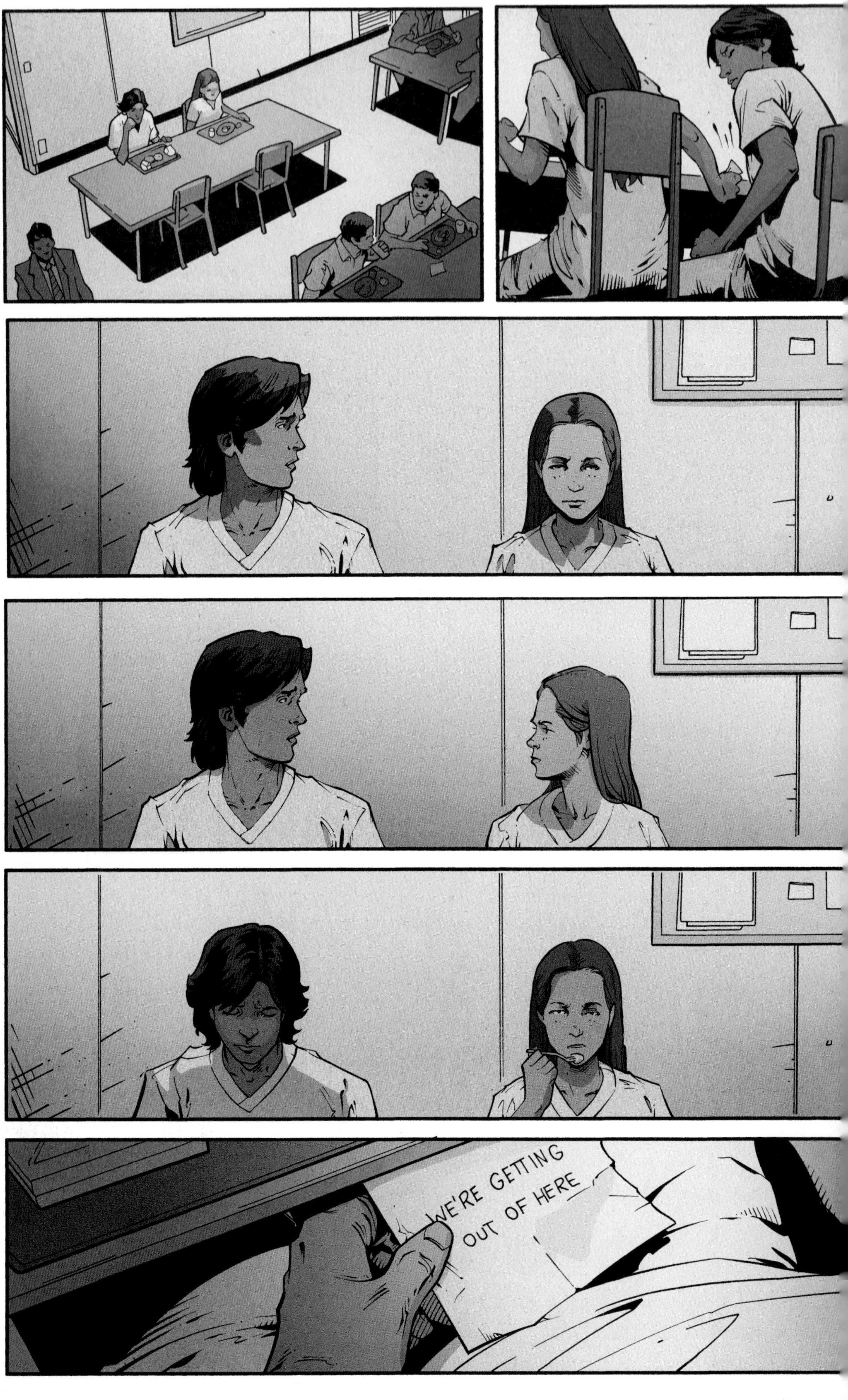
WE'RE GETTING OUT OF HERE

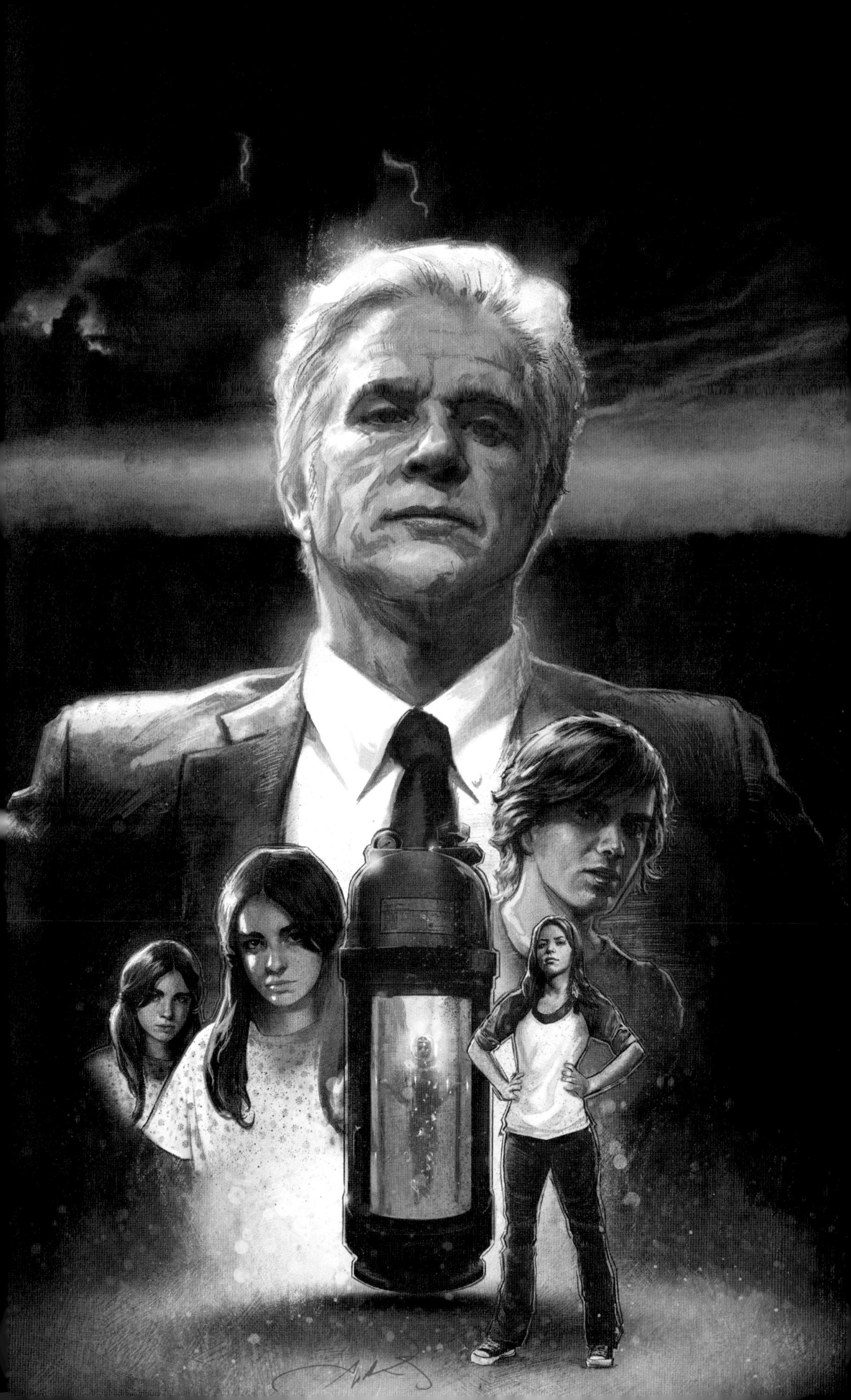

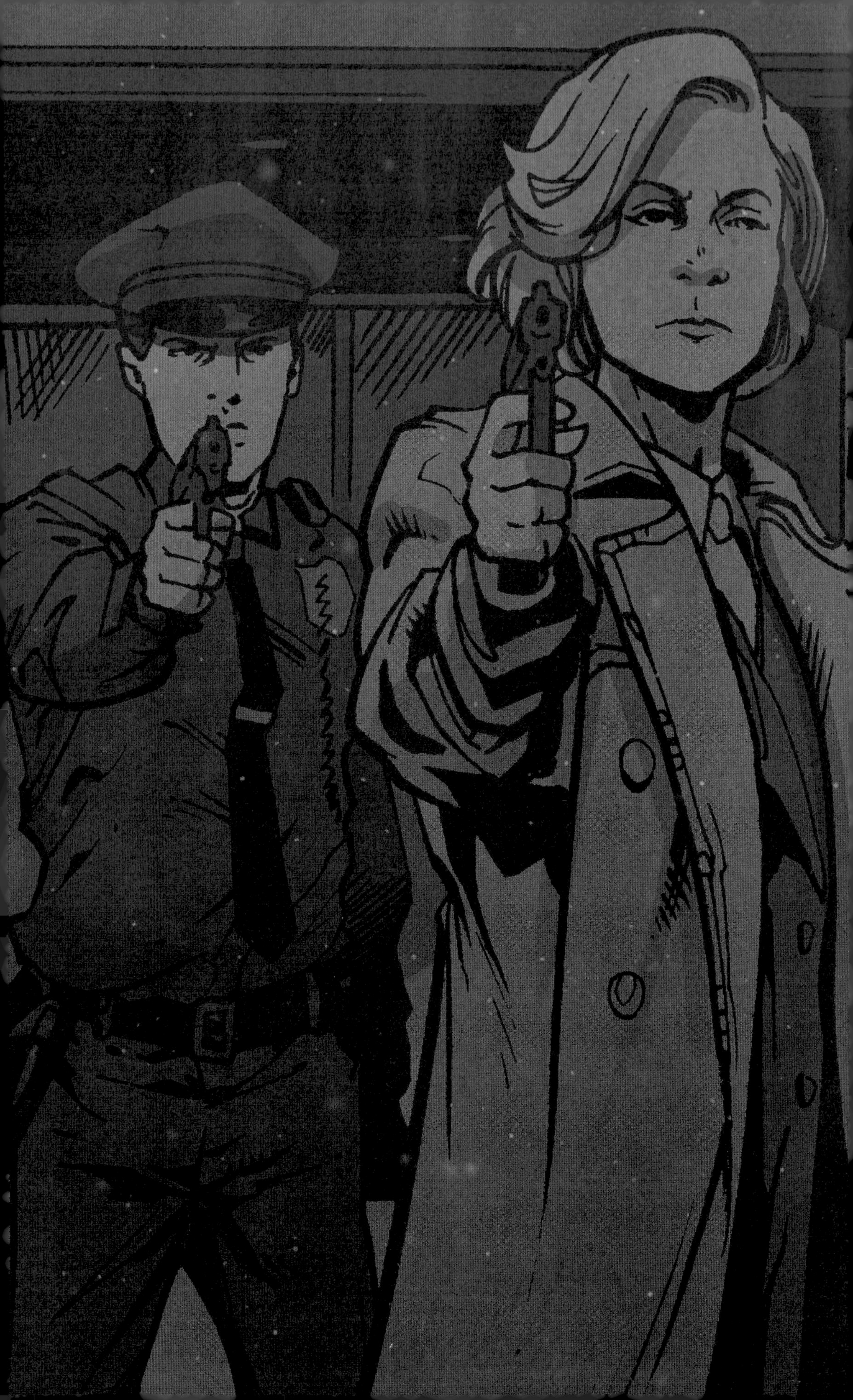

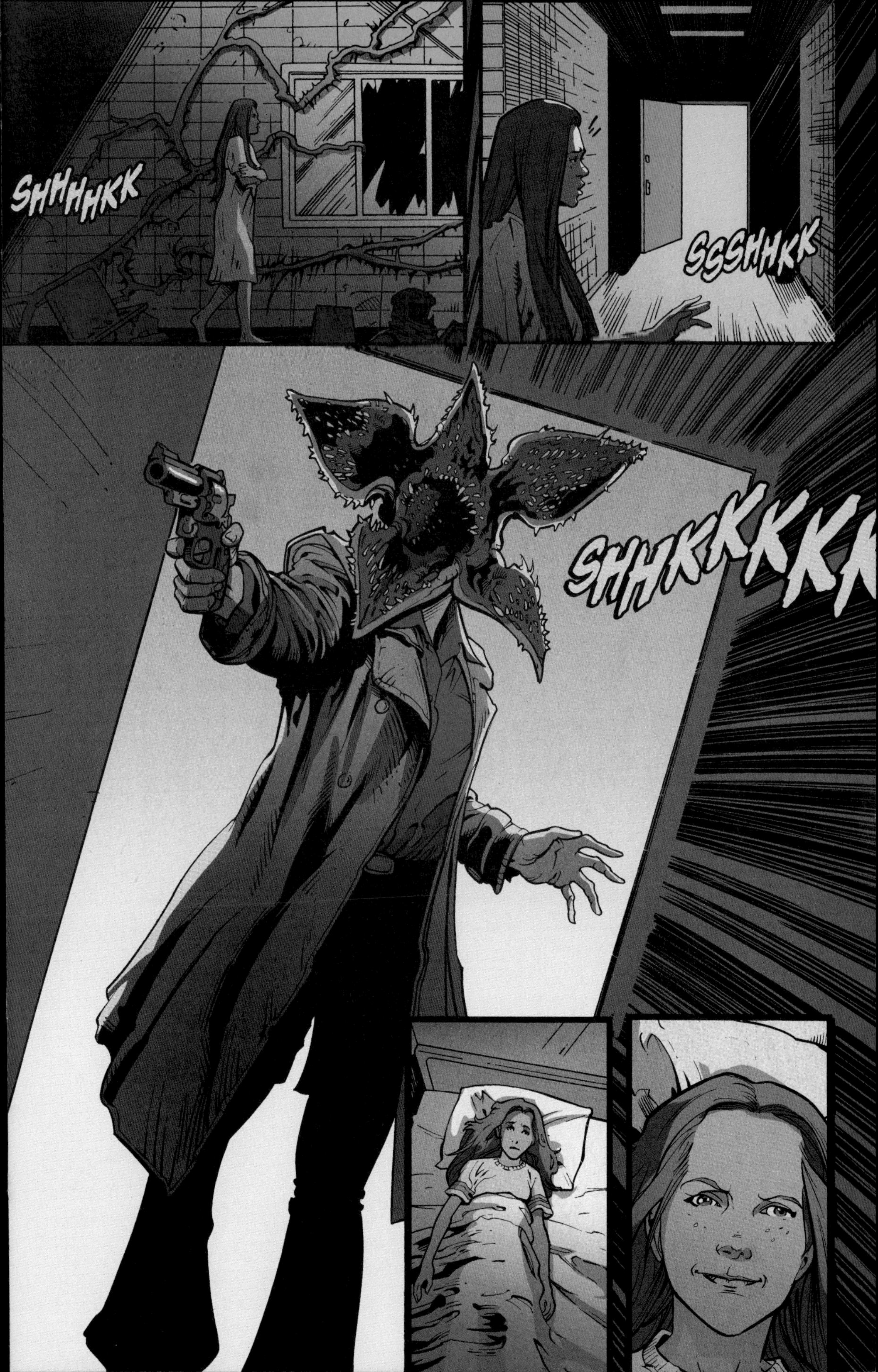
SHHHHKK
SSSHHKK
SHHKKKKK

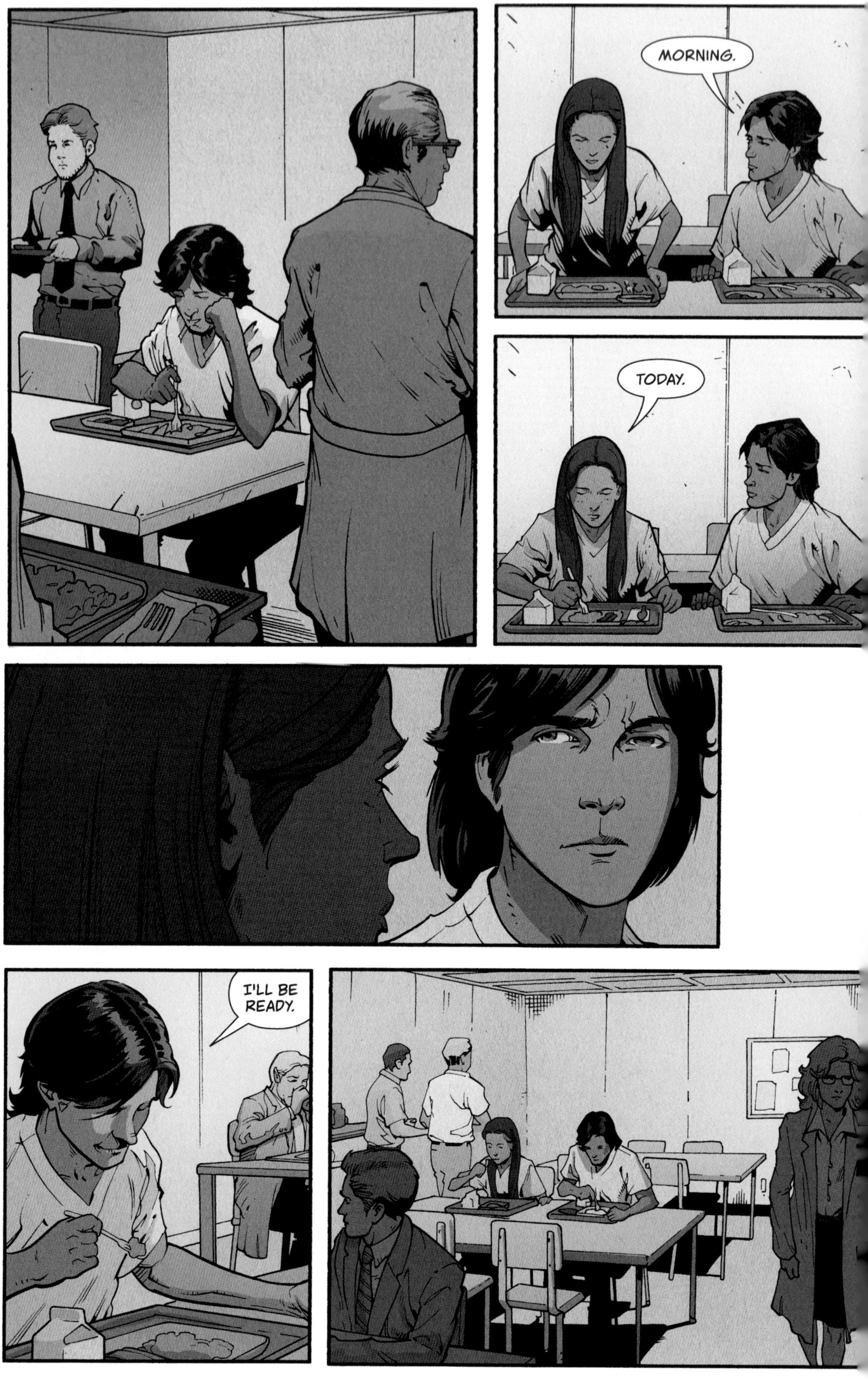
MORNING.
TODAY.
I'LL BE READY.

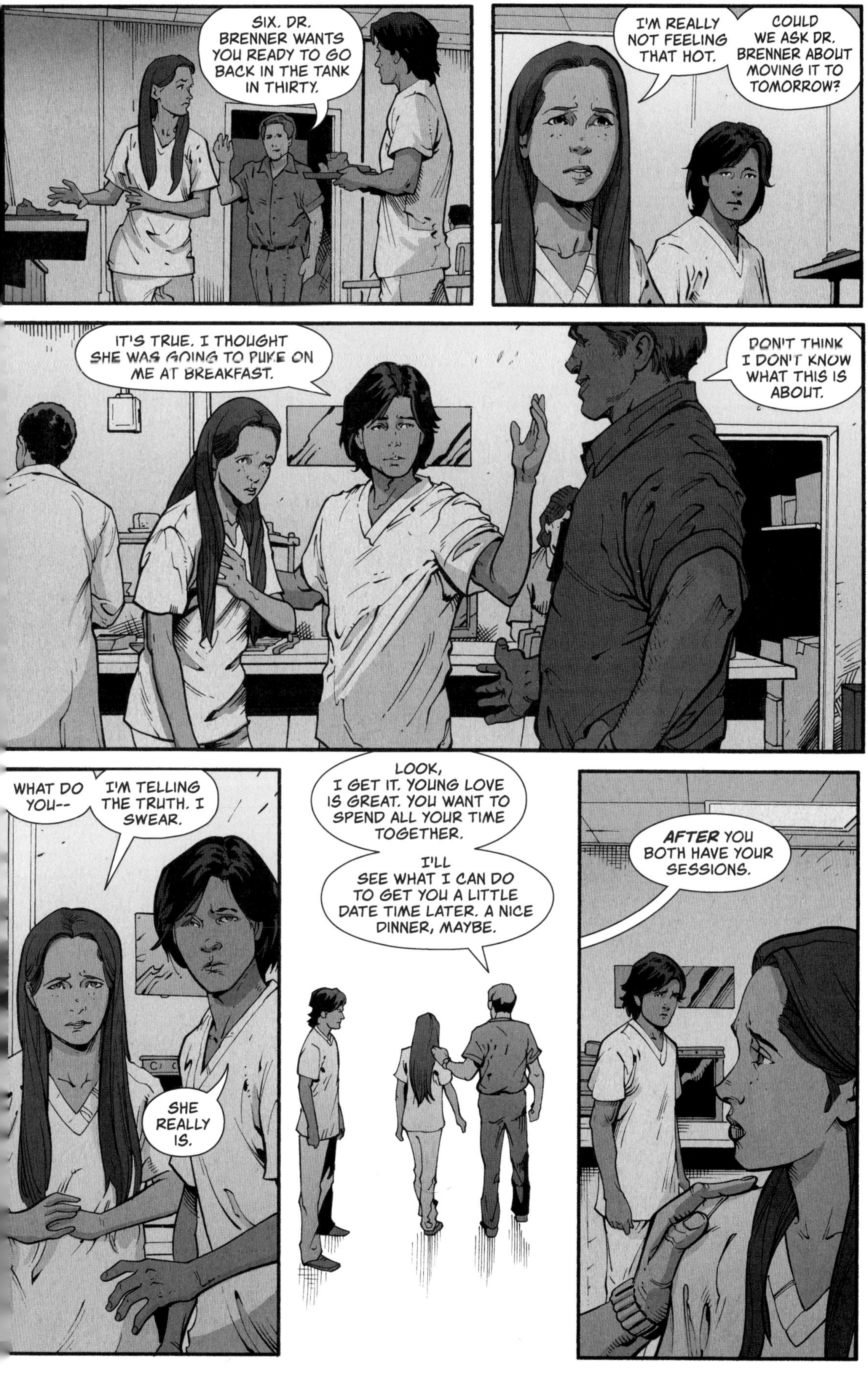
SIX. DR. BRENNER WANTS YOU READY TO GO BACK IN THE TANK IN THIRTY.
I'M REALLY NOT FEELING THAT HOT.
COULD WE ASK DR. BRENNER ABOUT MOVING IT TO TOMORROW?
IT'S TRUE. I THOUGHT SHE WAS GOING TO PUKE ON ME AT BREAKFAST.
DON'T THINK I DON'T KNOW WHAT THIS IS ABOUT.
WHAT DO YOU--
I'M TELLING THE TRUTH. I SWEAR.
SHE REALLY IS.
LOOK, I GET IT. YOUNG LOVE IS GREAT. YOU WANT TO SPEND ALL YOUR TIME TOGETHER.
I'LL SEE WHAT I CAN DO TO GET YOU A LITTLE DATE TIME LATER. A NICE DINNER, MAYBE.
AFTER YOU BOTH HAVE YOUR SESSIONS.

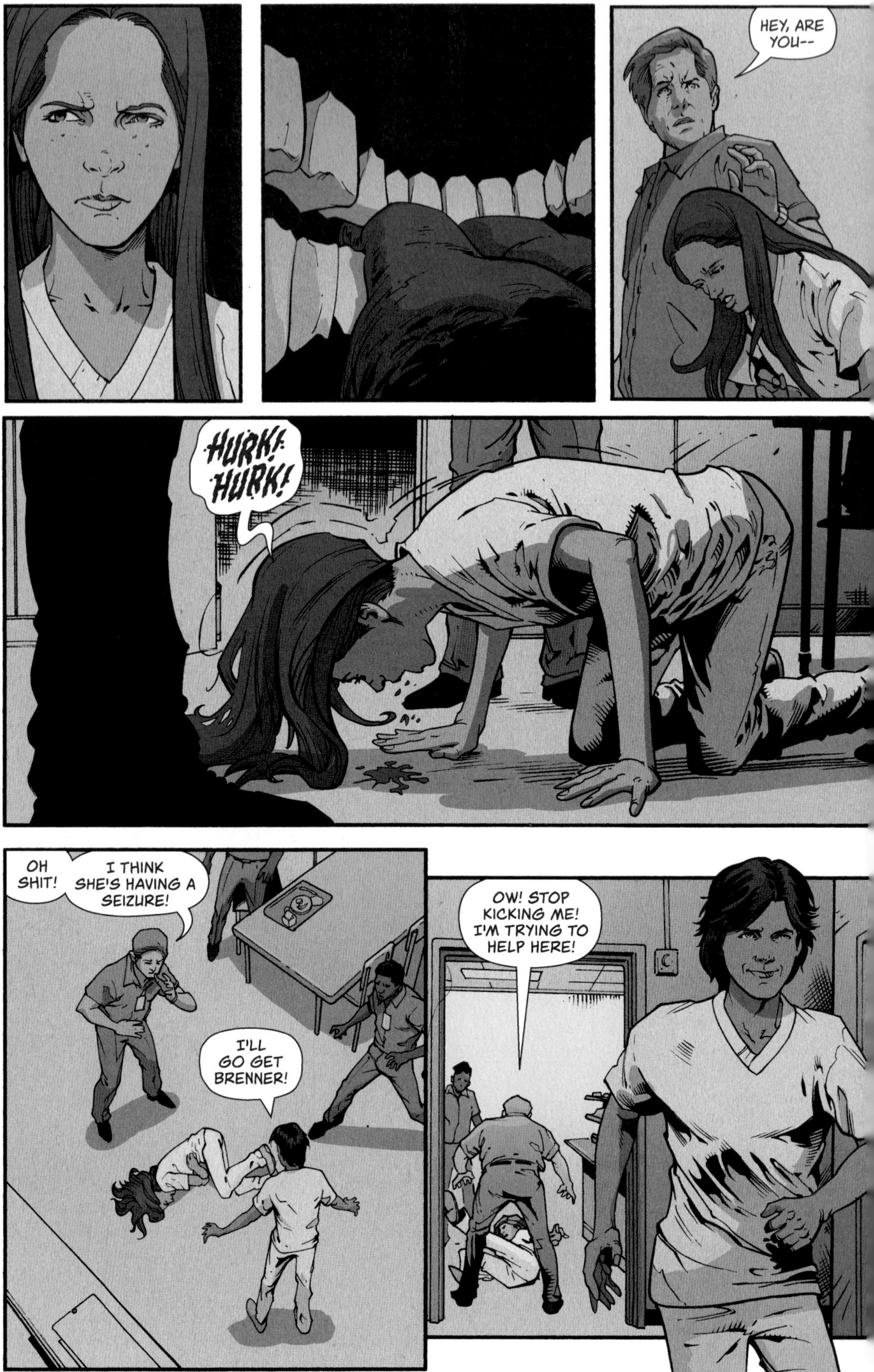
HEY, ARE YOU--
HURK! HURK!
OH SHIT!
I THINK SHE'S HAVING A SEIZURE!
I'LL GO GET BRENNER!
OW! STOP KICKING ME! I'M TRYING TO HELP HERE!

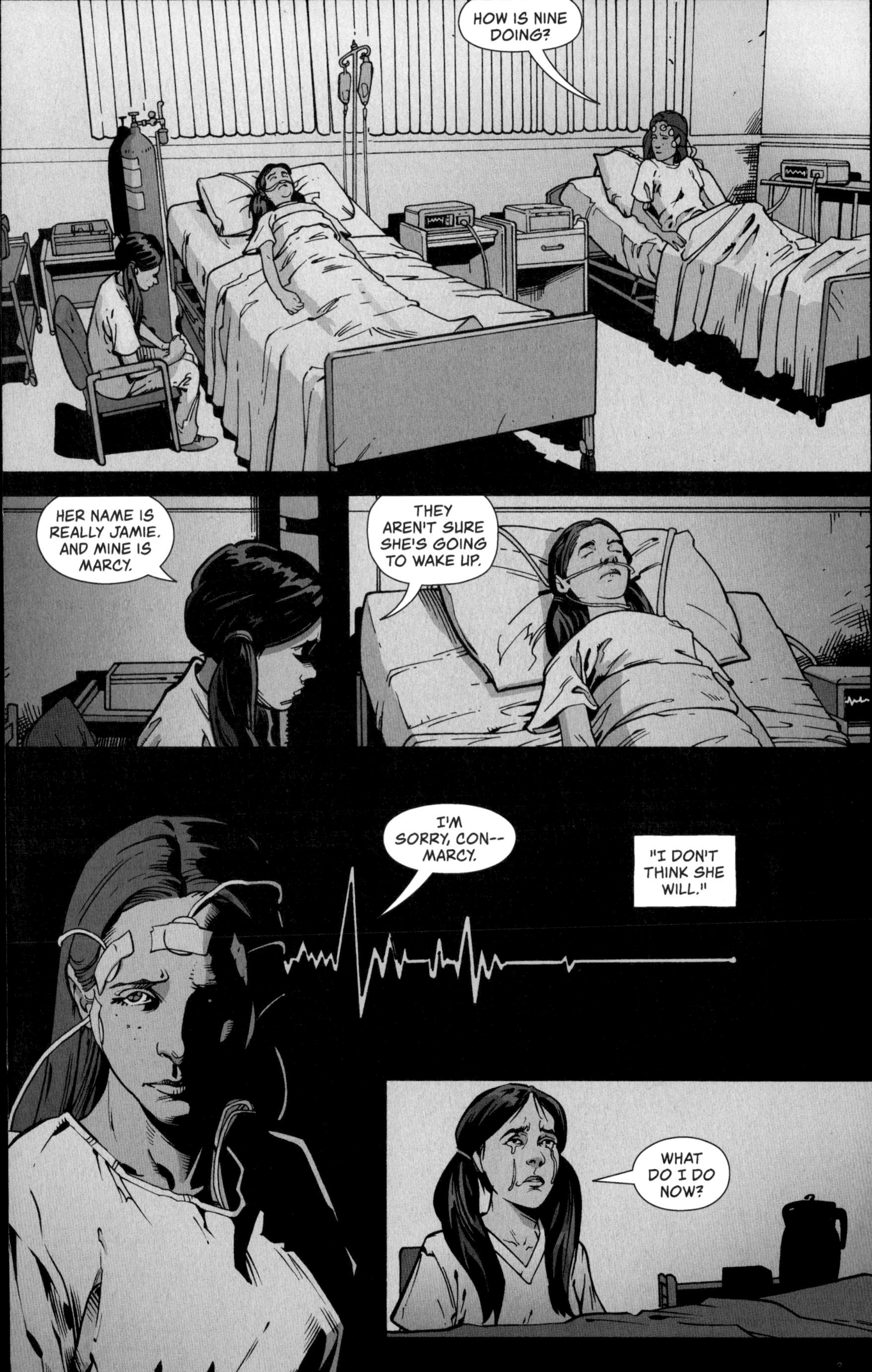
HOW IS NINE DOING?
HER NAME IS REALLY JAMIE. AND MINE IS MARCY.
THEY AREN'T SURE SHE'S GOING TO WAKE UP.
I'M SORRY, CON--MARCY.
"I DON'T THINK SHE WILL."
WHAT DO I DO NOW?

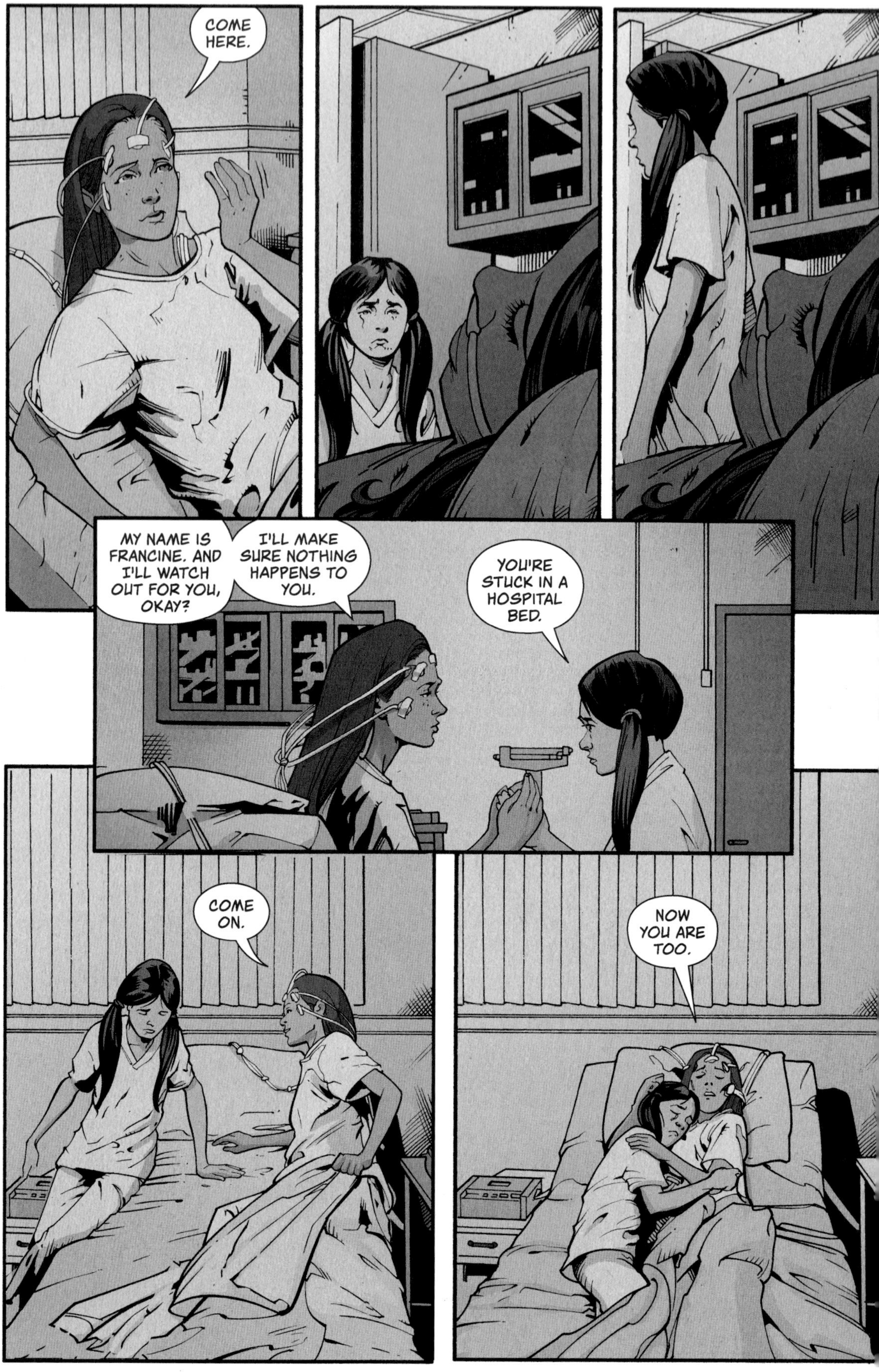
COME HERE.
MY NAME IS FRANCINE. AND I'LL WATCH OUT FOR YOU, OKAY?
I'LL MAKE SURE NOTHING HAPPENS TO YOU.
YOU'RE STUCK IN A HOSPITAL BED.
COME ON.
NOW YOU ARE TOO.

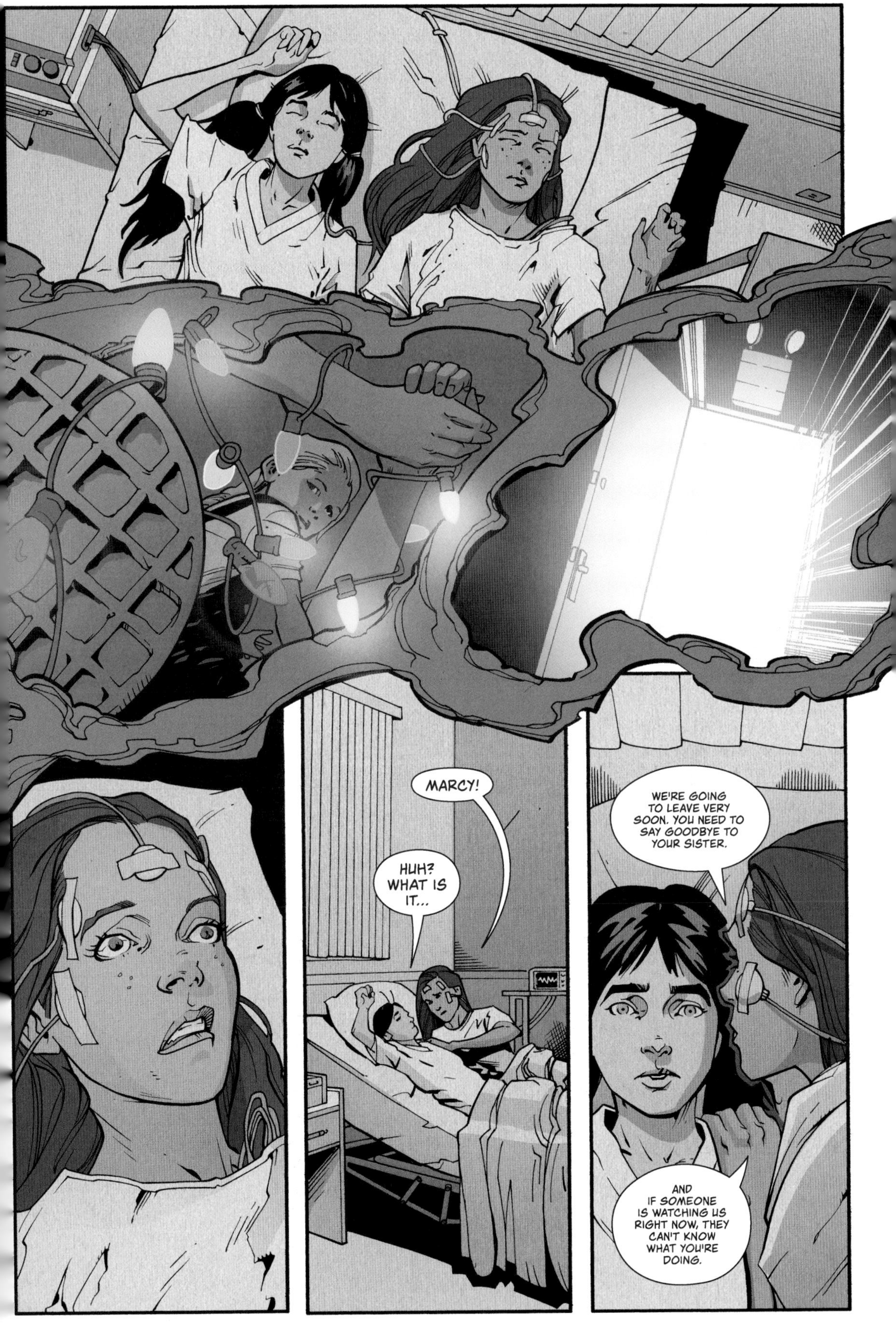
MARCY!
HUH? WHAT IS IT...
WE'RE GOING TO LEAVE VERY SOON. YOU NEED TO SAY GOODBYE TO YOUR SISTER.
AND IF SOMEONE IS WATCHING US RIGHT NOW, THEY CAN'T KNOW WHAT YOU'RE DOING.

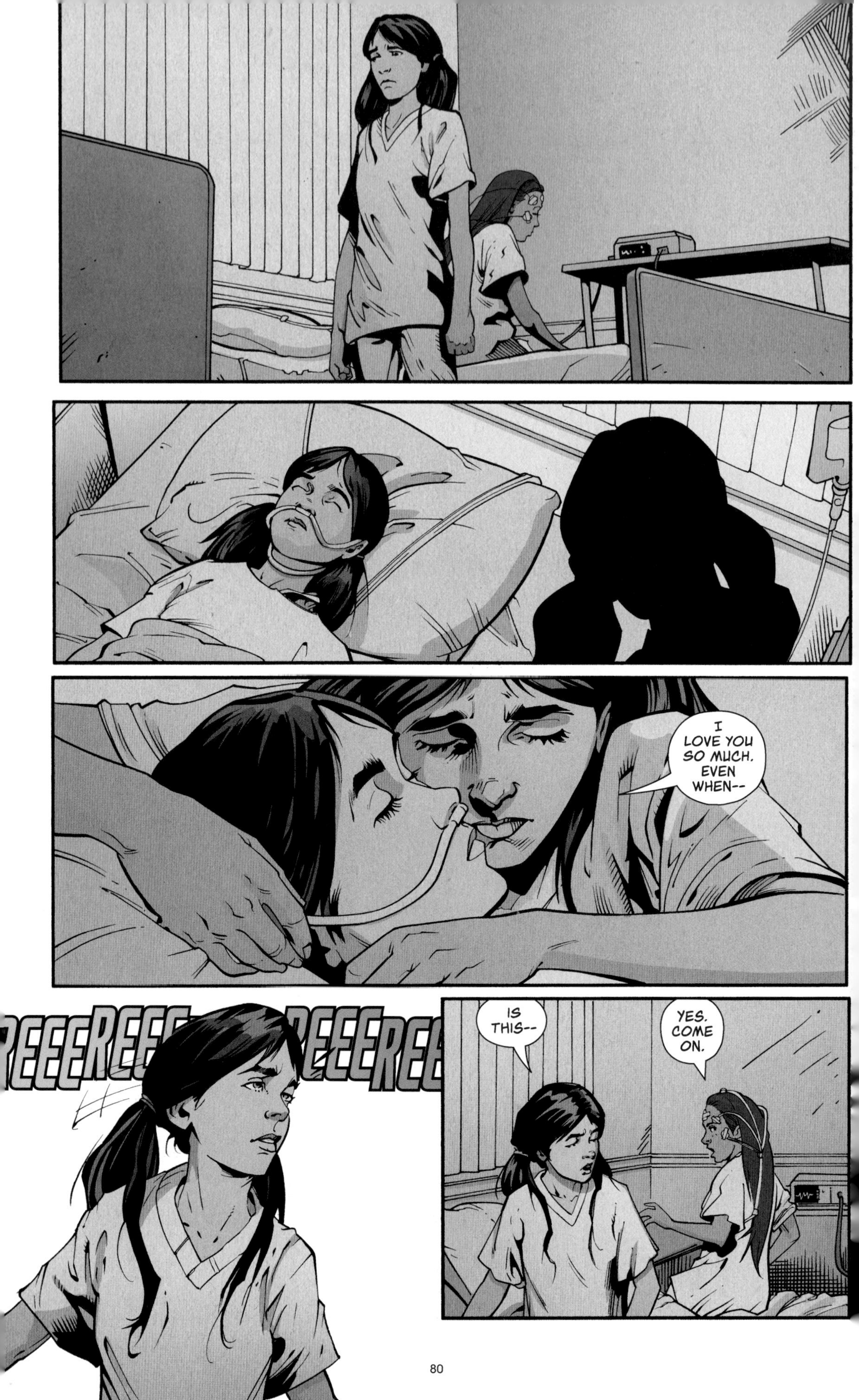
I LOVE YOU SO MUCH. EVEN WHEN--
REEEREEE
REEEREEE
IS THIS--
YES. COME ON.

REEEREEEREE
REEEREEEREE
COME ON! WE HAVE TO FIND RICKY!
SIX? FRANCINE?

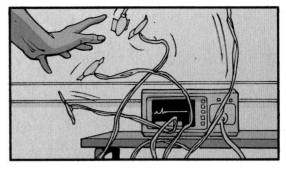

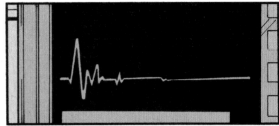

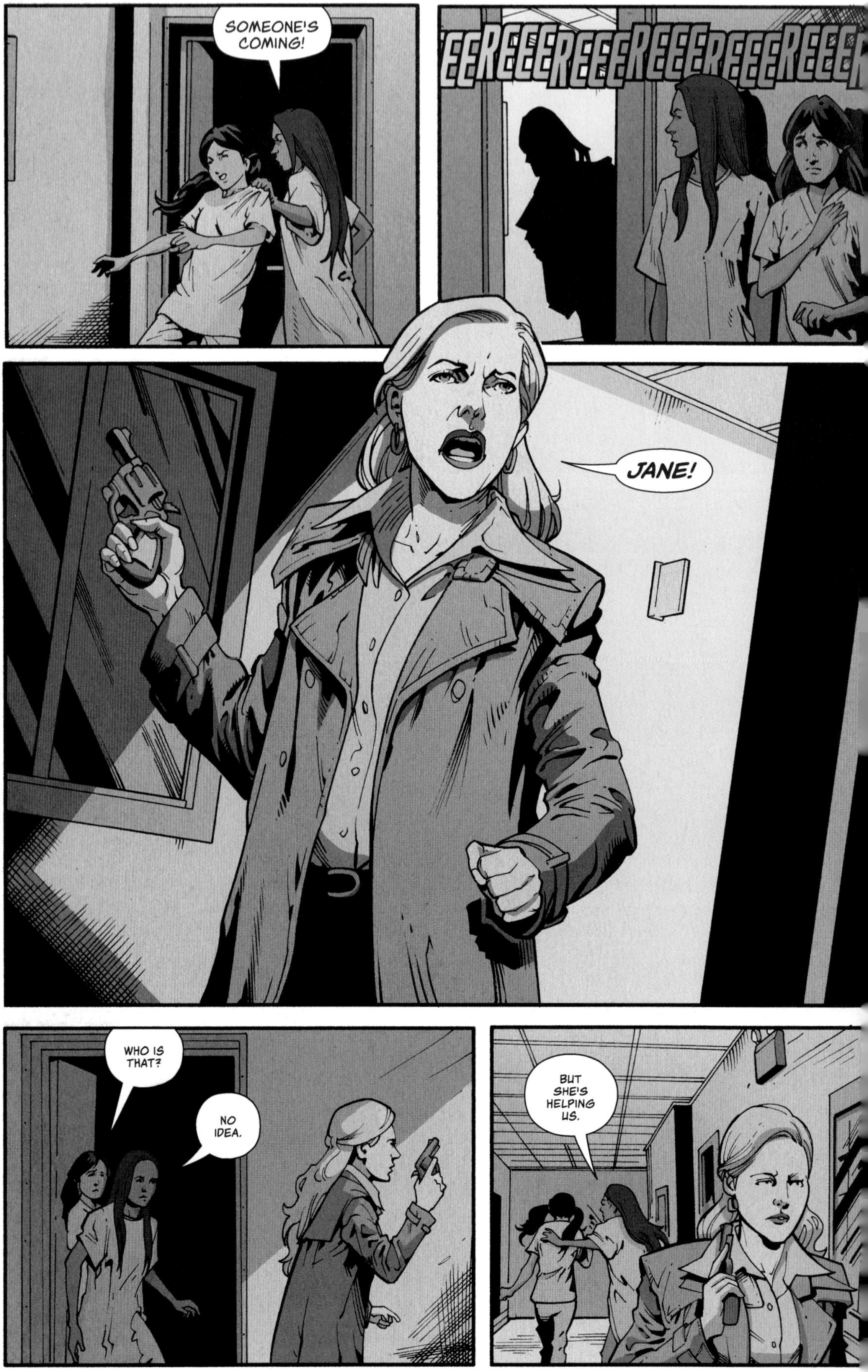
SOMEONE'S COMING!
EEREEEREEEREEEREEEREEER
JANE!
WHO IS THAT?
NO IDEA.
BUT SHE'S HELPING US.

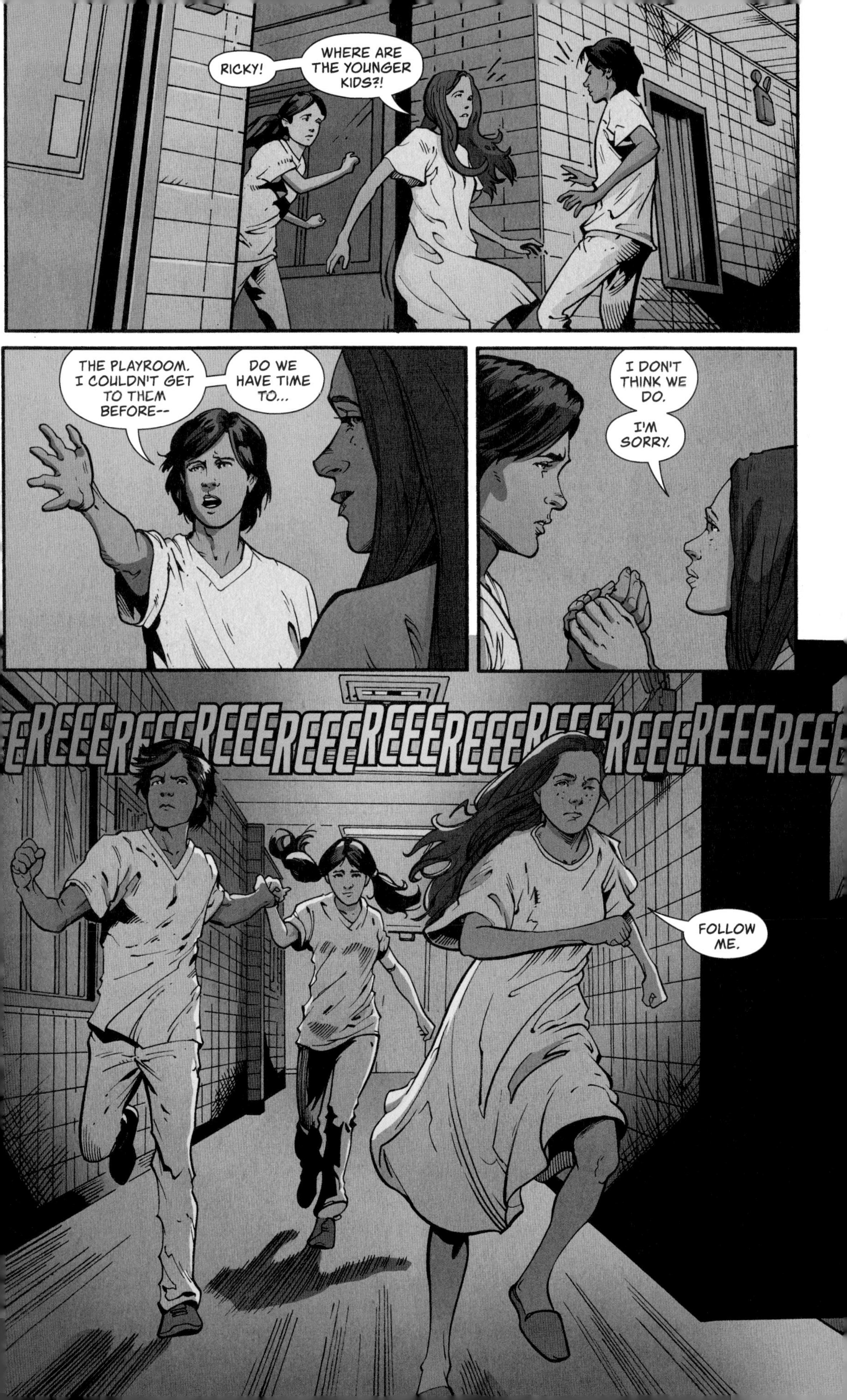
RICKY!
WHERE ARE THE YOUNGER KIDS?!
THE PLAYROOM. I COULDN'T GET TO THEM BEFORE--
DO WE HAVE TIME TO...
I DON'T THINK WE DO.
I'M SORRY.
REEEREEEREEEREEEREEEREEEREEEREEEREEEREEEREEE
FOLLOW ME.

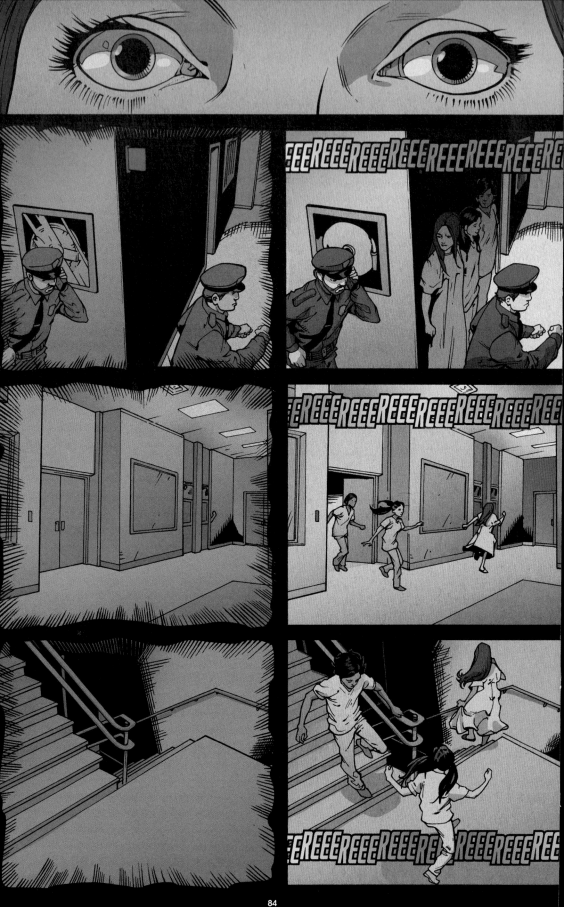

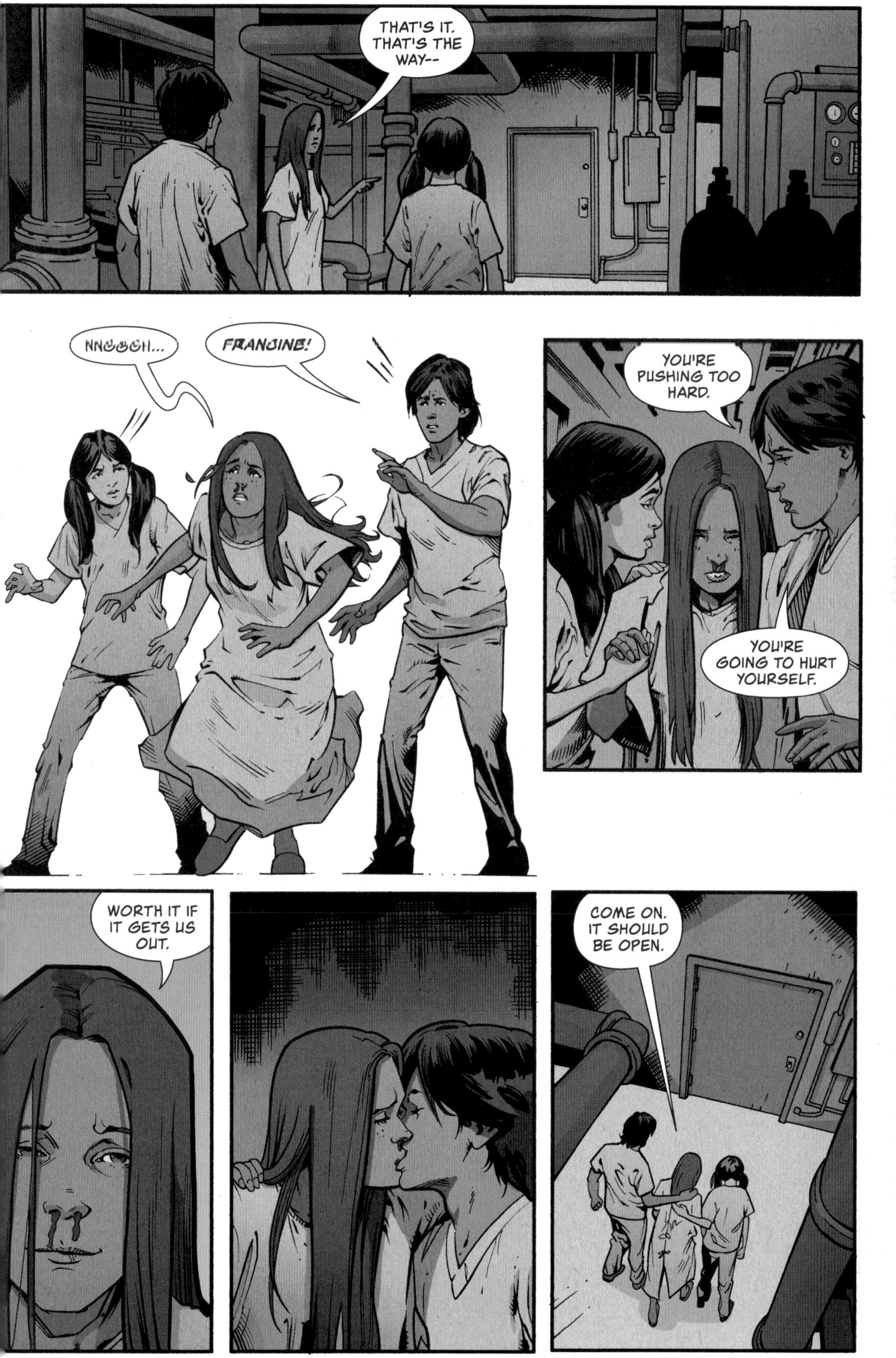
THAT'S IT. THAT'S THE WAY--
NNGGGH...
FRANCINE!
YOU'RE PUSHING TOO HARD.
YOU'RE GOING TO HURT YOURSELF.
WORTH IT IF IT GETS US OUT.
COME ON. IT SHOULD BE OPEN.

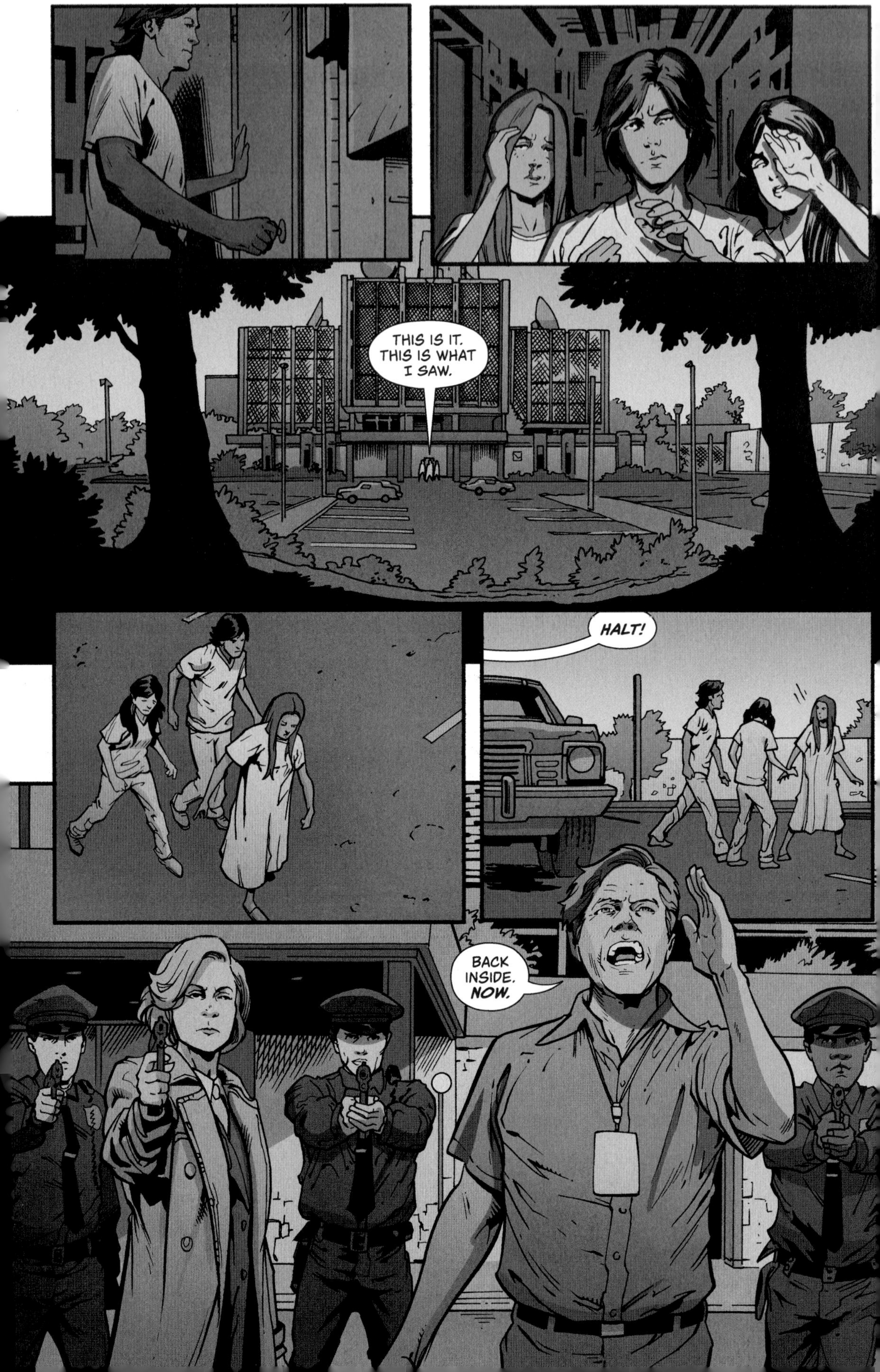
THIS IS IT. THIS IS WHAT I SAW.
HALT!
BACK INSIDE. NOW.

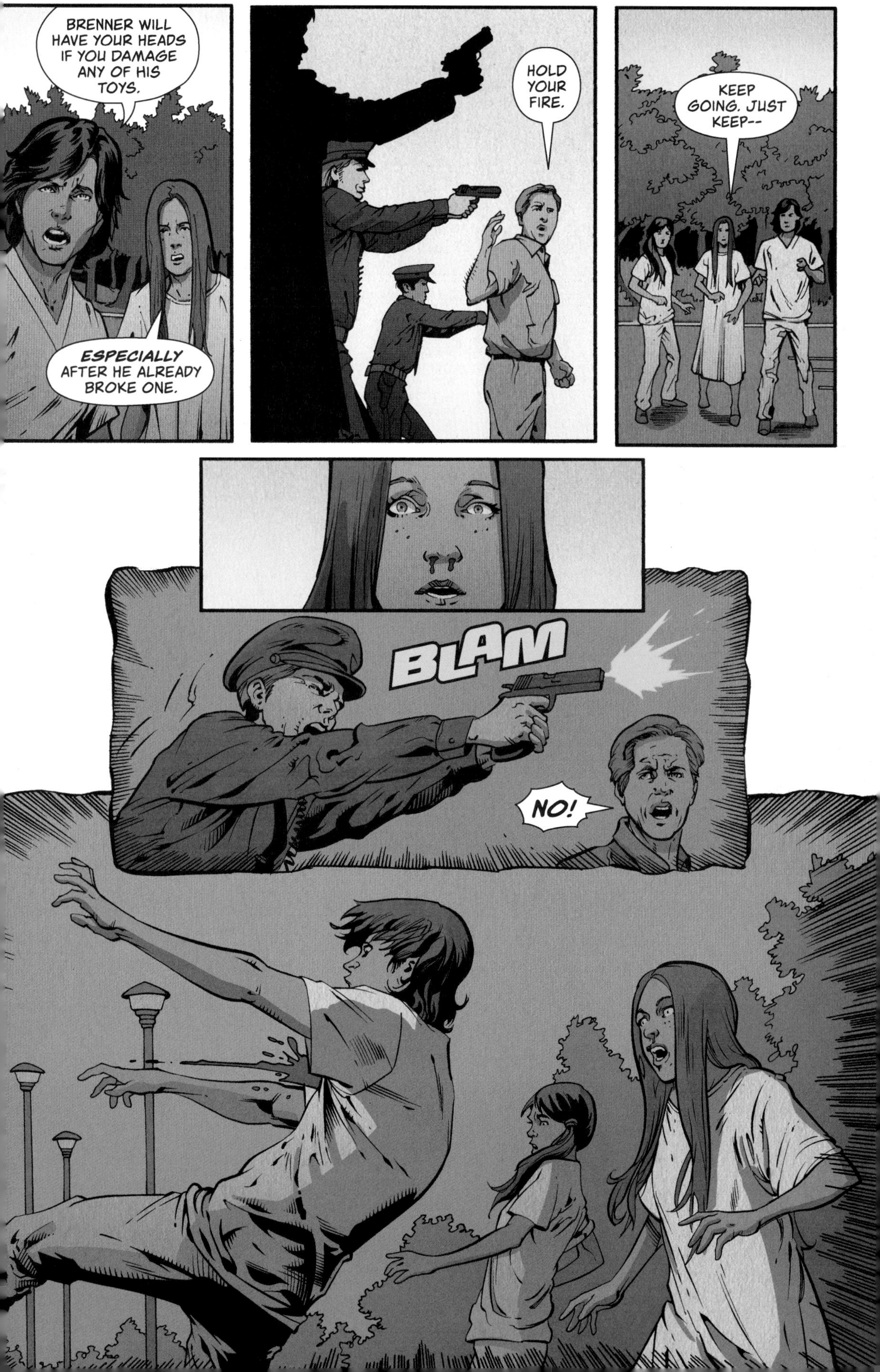
BRENNER WILL HAVE YOUR HEADS IF YOU DAMAGE ANY OF HIS TOYS.
ESPECIALLY AFTER HE ALREADY BROKE ONE.
HOLD YOUR FIRE.
KEEP GOING. JUST KEEP--
BLAM
NO!

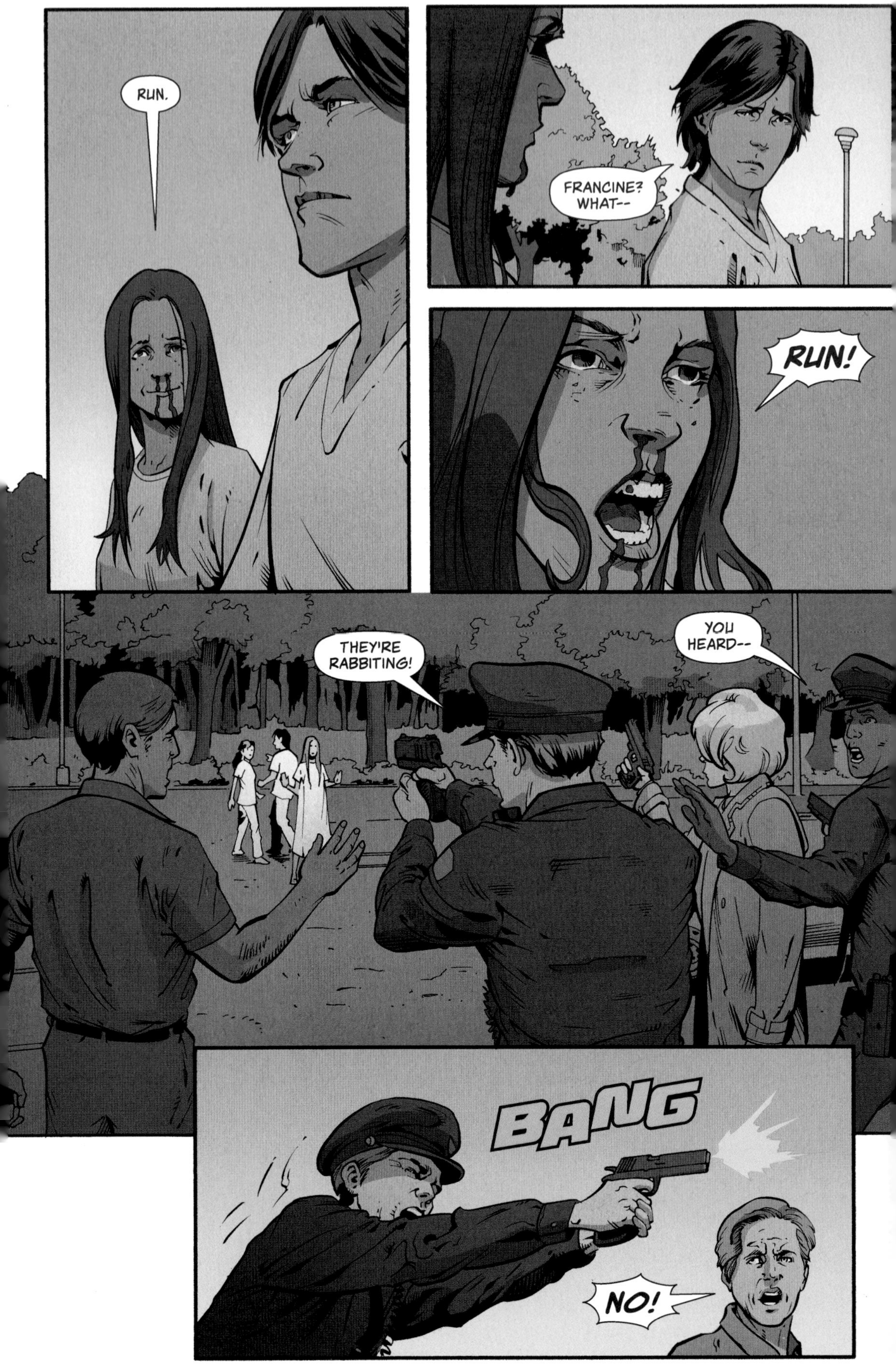
RUN.
FRANCINE? WHAT--
RUN!
THEY'RE RABBITING!
YOU HEARD--
BANG
NO!

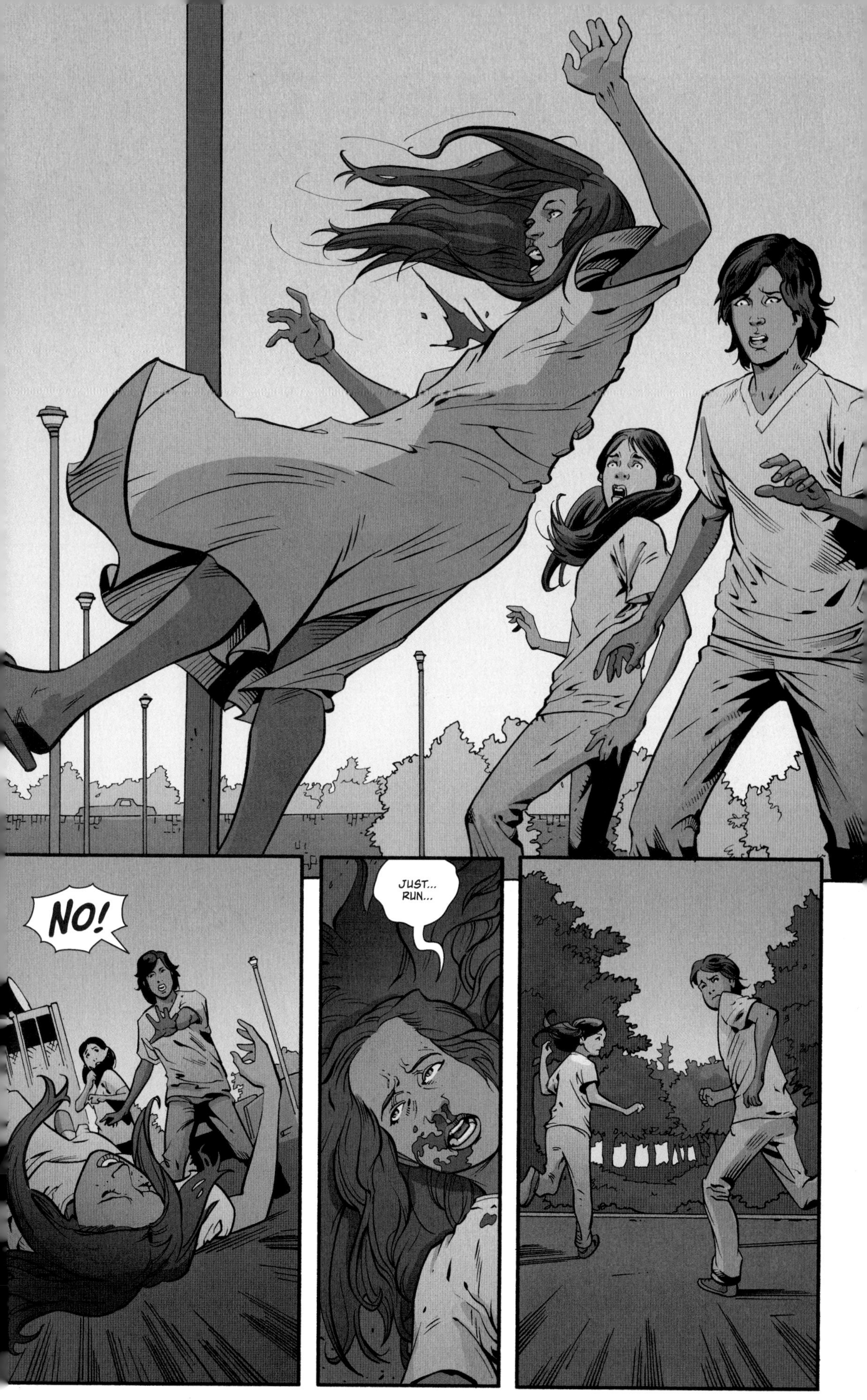
NO!
JUST... RUN...

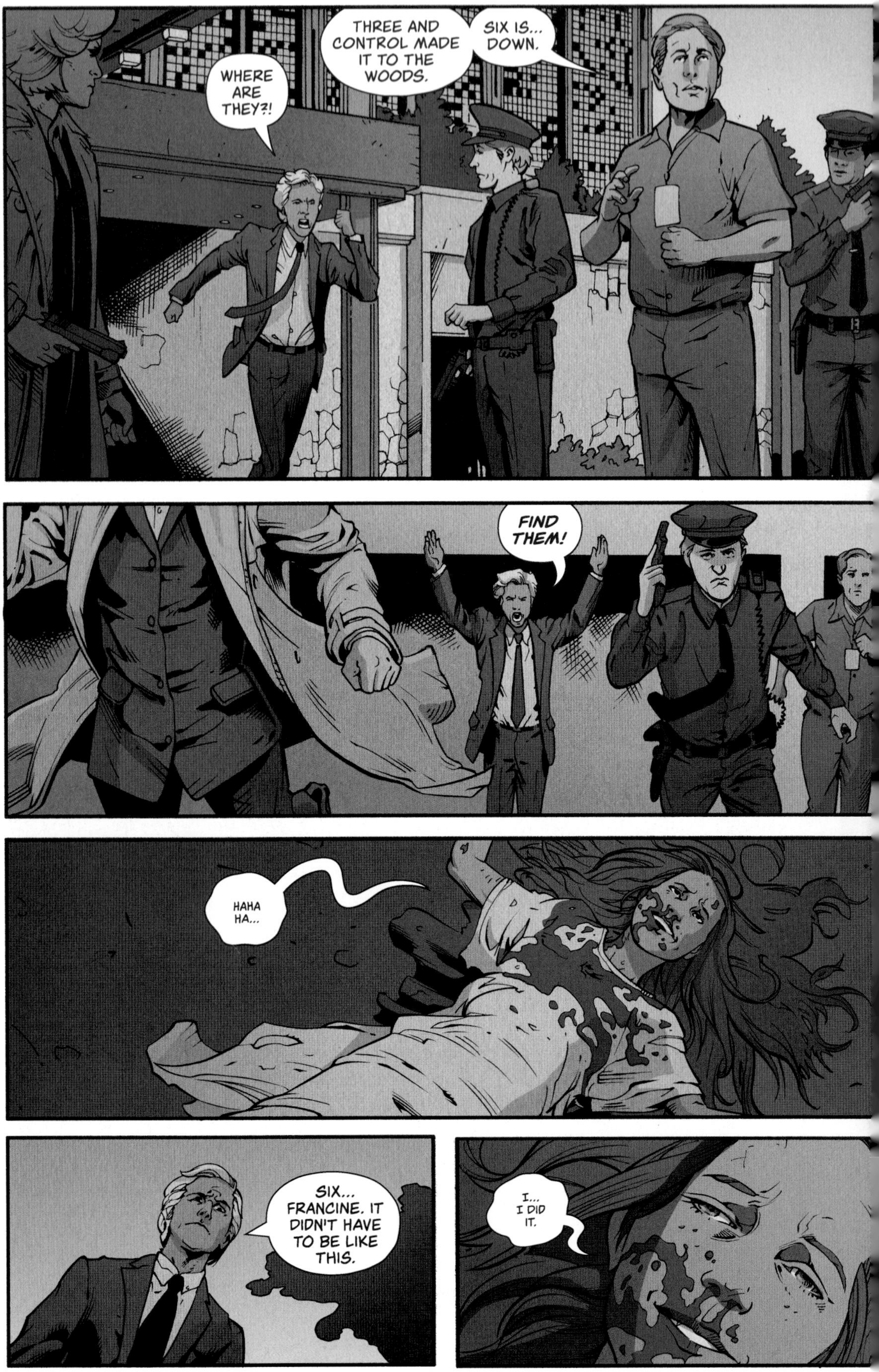
WHERE ARE THEY?!
THREE AND CONTROL MADE IT TO THE WOODS.
SIX IS... DOWN.
FIND THEM!
HAHA HA...
SIX... FRANCINE. IT DIDN'T HAVE TO BE LIKE THIS.
I... I DID IT.

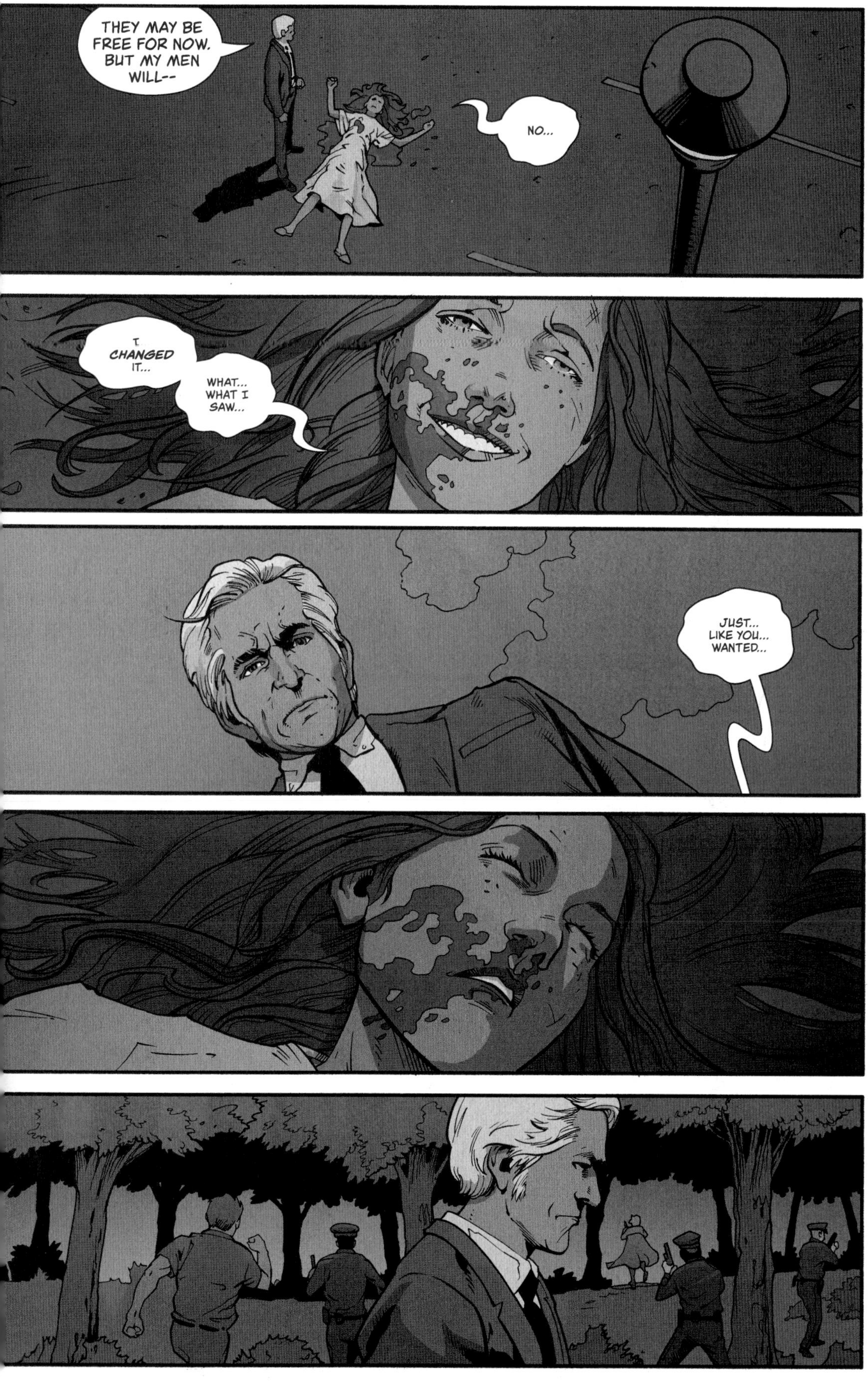
THEY MAY BE FREE FOR NOW. BUT MY MEN WILL--
NO...
I CHANGED IT...
WHAT... WHAT I SAW...
JUST... LIKE YOU... WANTED...

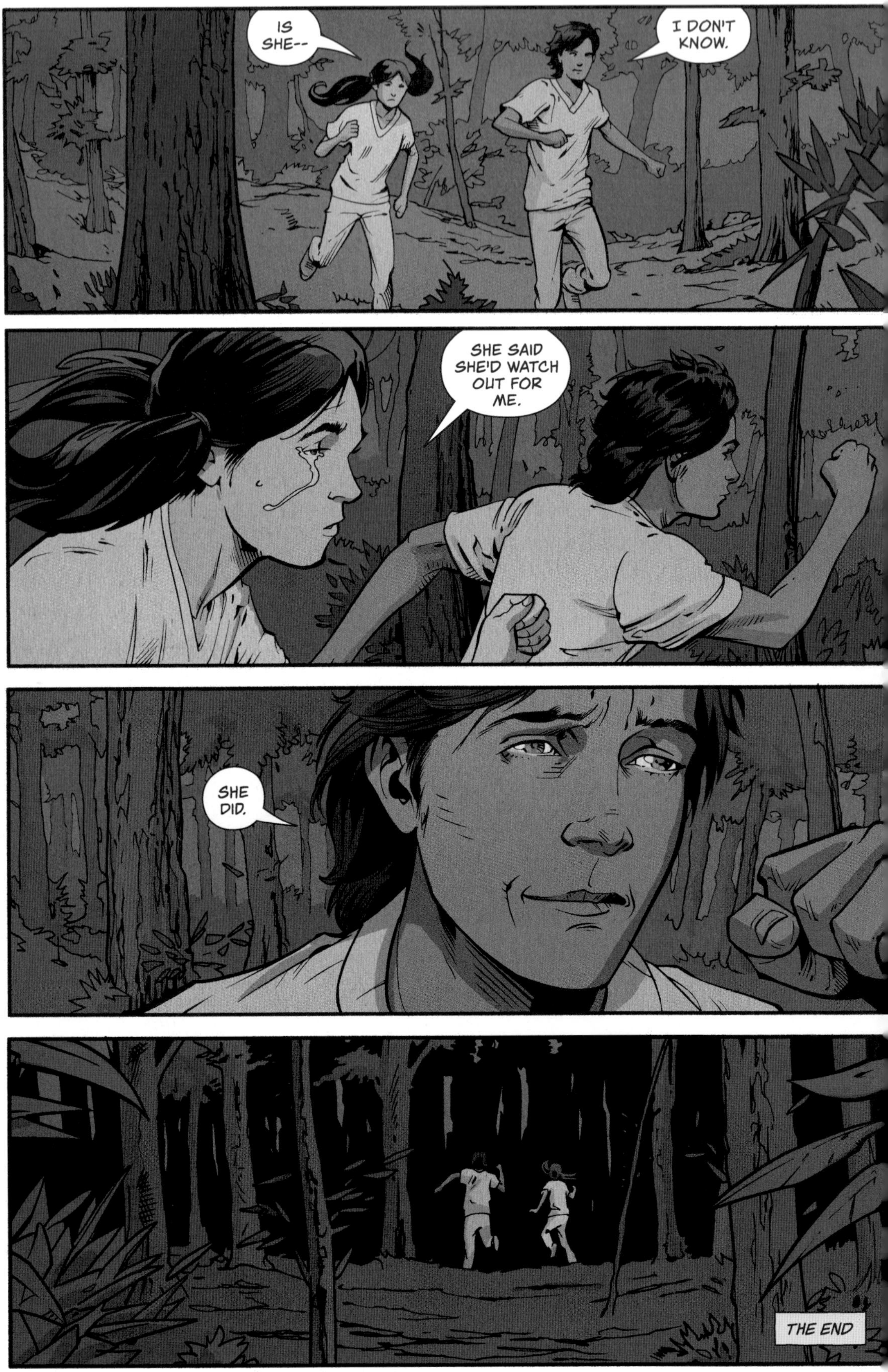
IS SHE--
I DON'T KNOW.
SHE SAID SHE'D WATCH OUT FOR ME.
SHE DID.
THE END

llustration by DAVID MACK

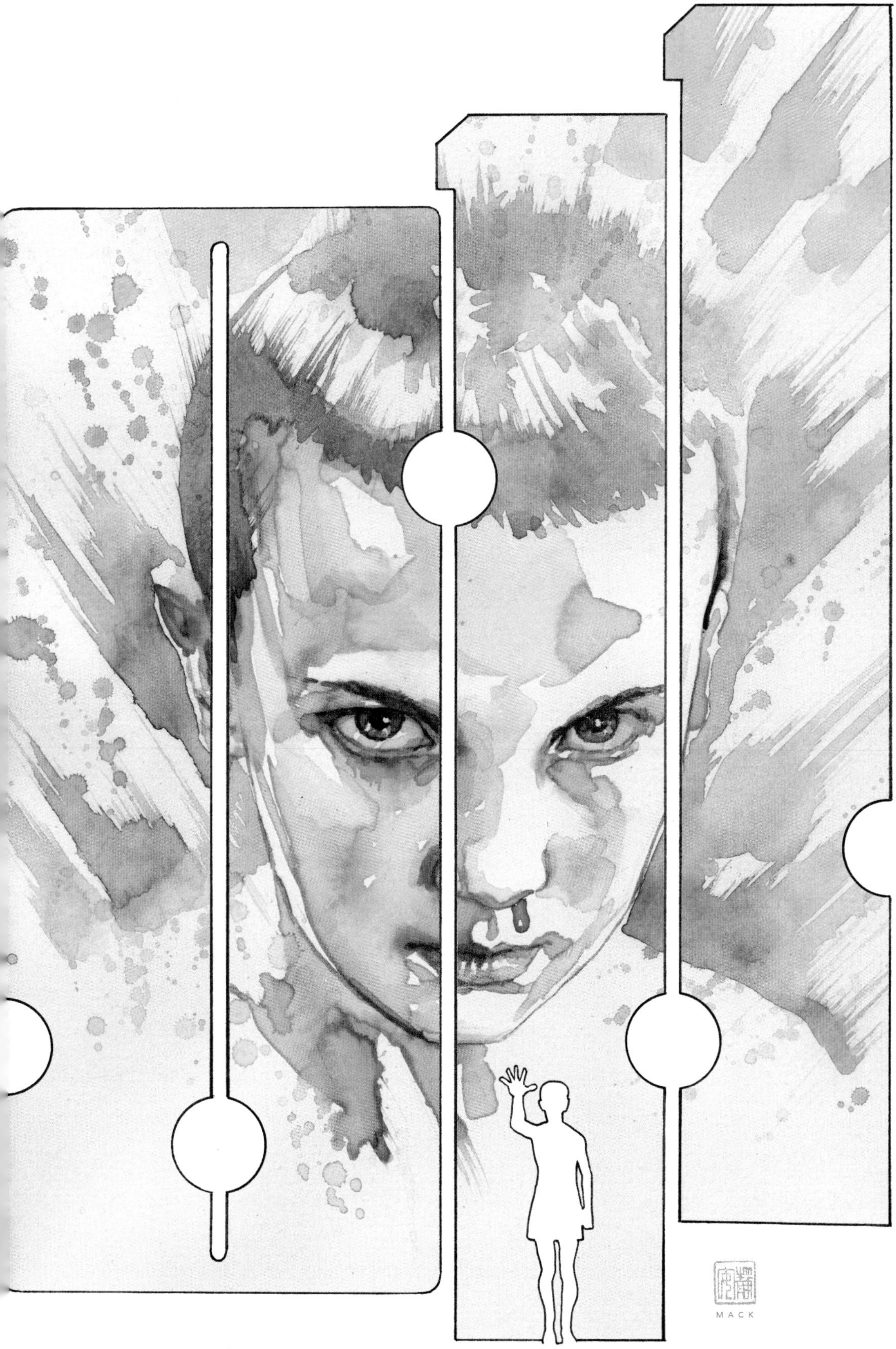
MACK

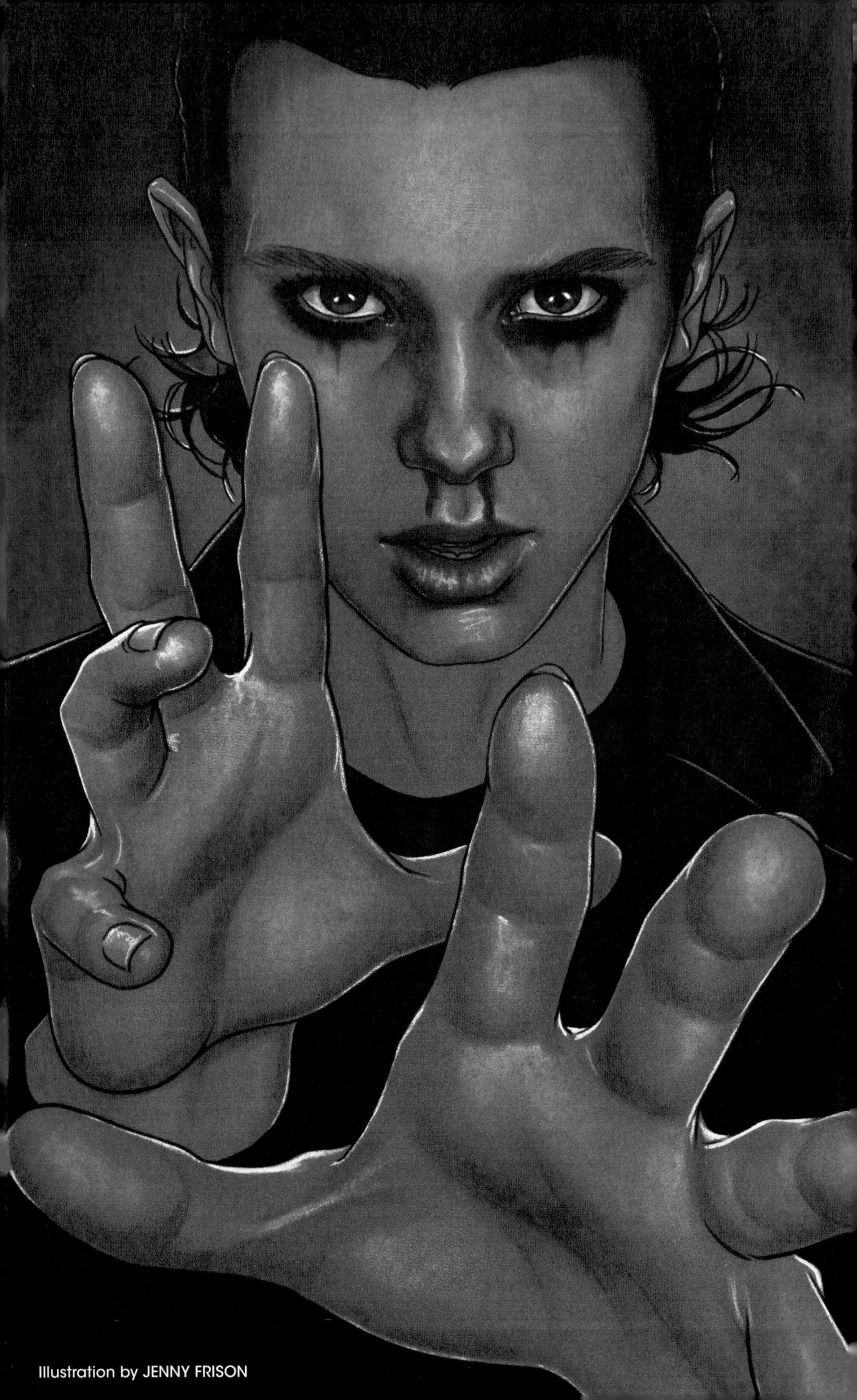

Illustration by JENNY FRISON

STRANGER THINGS

THE NOSTALGIA-IGNITING HIT NETFLIX ORIGINAL SERIES COMES TO COMICS!

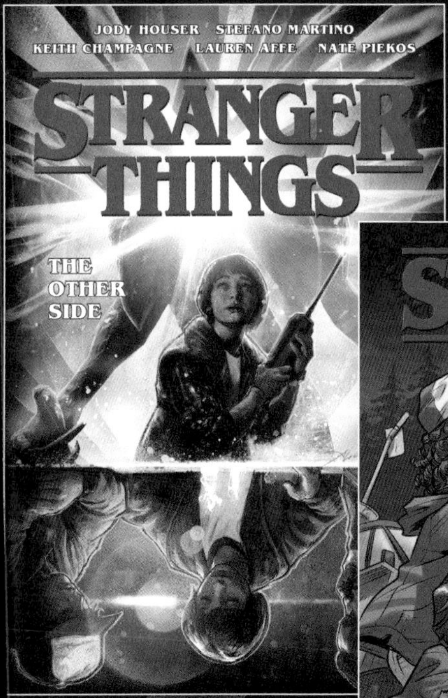
JODY HOUSER STEFANO MARTINO
KEITH CHAMPAGNE LAUREN AFFE NATE PIEKOS
STRANGER THINGS
THE OTHER SIDE

VOLUME 1: THE OTHER SIDE
Jody Houser, Stefano Martino, Keith Champagne, Lauren Affe
ISBN 978-1-50670-976-5
$17.99

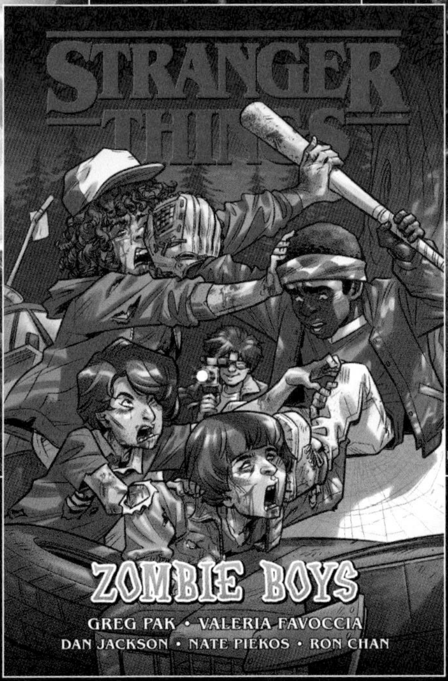
STRANGER THINGS
ZOMBIE BOYS
GREG PAK • VALERIA FAVOCCIA
DAN JACKSON • NATE PIEKOS • RON CHAN

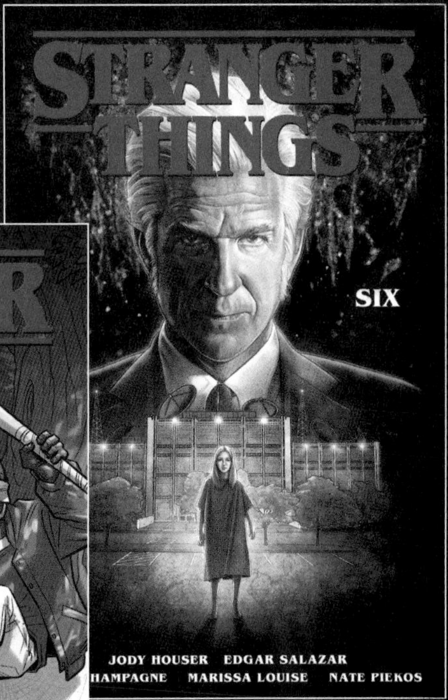
STRANGER THINGS
SIX
JODY HOUSER EDGAR SALAZAR
MARISSA LOUISE NATE PIEKOS

VOLUME 2: SIX
Jody Houser, Edgar Salazar, Keith Champagne, Marissa Louise
ISBN 978-1-50671-232-1
$17.99

ZOMBIE BOYS
Greg Pak, Valeria Favoccia, Dan Jackson
ISBN 978-1-50671-309-0
$10.99

DARKHORSE.COM • AVAILABLE AT YOUR LOCAL COMICS SHOP OR BOOKSTORE
To find a comics shop near you, visit comicshoplocator.com
For more information or to order direct, visit darkhorse.com

NETFLIX

GERARD WAY

"...[F]lawless... stylish, imaginative..." —NEWSARAMA

THE UMBRELLA ACADEMY™

Written by **GERARD WAY**
Art by **GABRIEL BÁ**
Featuring covers by **JAMES JEAN**

The seven adopted children of Sir Reginald Hargreeves form the Umbrella Academy, a dysfunctional family of superheroes with bizarre powers. These disgruntled siblings are the only ones who can save the world from robot assassins, fashionable terrorists, and their own worst impulses! Now a live-action series from Netflix!

"It's the X-Men for cool people." —GRANT MORRISON (*ALL STAR SUPERMAN*)

VOLUME 1: APOCALYPSE SUITE LIBRARY EDITION HARDCOVER
ISBN 978-1-50671-547-6
$39.99

VOLUME 1: APOCALYPSE SUITE
ISBN 978-1-59307-978-9
$17.99

VOLUME 2: DALLAS
ISBN 978-1-59582-345-8
$17.99

VOLUME 3: HOTEL OBLIVION
ISBN 978-1-50671-142-3
$17.99

THE UMBRELLA ACADEMY JOURNAL
$19.99
NOV180283

THE UMBRELLA ACADEMY PLAYING CARDS
$4.99
DEC180427

THE UMBRELLA ACADEMY MAGNET 4-PACK
$9.99
NOV180279

THE UMBRELLA ACADEMY: APOCALYPSE SUITE PUZZLE
$19.99
DEC180426

THE UMBRELLA ACADEMY "WHEN EVIL RAINS" MUG
NOV180282
$12.99

THE UMBRELLA ACADEMY HAZEL AND CHA CHA MUG
APR190333
$12.99

THE UMBRELLA ACADEMY ENAMEL PIN SET
$14.99
NOV180281

THE UMBRELLA ACADEMY COASTER SET
$9.99
NOV180280

THE UMBRELLA ACADEMY HAZEL AND CHA CHA PINT GLASS SET
APR190334
$19.99

Killjoys
The True Lives of the Fabulous™

Written by **GERARD WAY** & **SHAUN SIMON**
Art by **BECKY CLOONAN** & **DAN JACKSON**

Over a decade ago, a team of revolutionaries called the Killjoys lost their lives while saving a mysterious young girl from the tyrannical megacorporation Better Living Industries. Today, the Killjoys live on in memory, if not belief, as BLI widens its reach and freedom fades. The Girl, now grown, reemerges and is put in the spotlight as a savior, a role she knows nothing about. But with the new revolution hell bent on body counts, the Girl must look within herself to put an end to BLI once and for all.

"Uniquely refreshing." —**IGN**

TRADE PAPERBACK
ISBN 978-1-59582-462-2
$19.99

AVAILABLE AT YOUR LOCAL COMICS SHOP OR BOOKSTORE

To find a comics shop in your area, visit comicshoplocator.com. For more information or to order direct: On the web: darkhorse.com / E-mail: mailorder@darkhorse.com
Phone: 1-800-862-0052 Mon.–Fri. 9 a.m. to 5 p.m. Pacific Time.